How to Run your Charity

How to Run your Charity

The Role of the Charity Secretary

Malcolm Leatherdale LLB ACIS Solicitor

ICSA Publishing
*The Official Publishing Company of
The Institute of Chartered Secretaries and Administrators*

With

PRENTICE HALL EUROPE
London   New York   Toronto   Sydney   Tokyo   Singapore
Madrid   Mexico City   Munich   Paris

First published 1998 by
ICSA Publishing Limited
with Prentice Hall Europe
Campus 400, Maylands Avenue
Hemel Hempstead
Hertfordshire, HP2 7EZ

© ICSA Publishing Ltd 1998

All rights reserved. No part of this publication may be reproduced, stored in a retrieval system, or transmitted, in any form, or by any means, electronic, mechanical, photocopying, recording or otherwise, without prior permission, in writing, from the publisher.

Typeset in 10/12pt Palatino
by Dorwyn Ltd, Rowlands Castle, Hants

Printed and bound in Great Britain
by MPG Books, Bodmin, Cornwall

British Library Cataloguing in Publication Data

A catalogue record for this book is available from the British Library

ISBN: 1-860720-53-6

1 2 3 4 5   02 01 00 99 98

CONTENTS

Introduction   1

1.   The role and core duties of the charity secretary   3

1.1   The need for competent administration   3
1.2   The role of the secretary   4
1.3   The core duties and responsibilities of the secretary   5

2.   Compliance and the law   11

2.1   General compliance   11
2.2   Compliance with charities legislation   12
2.3   Compliance with companies legislation   15
2.4   Additional requirements to be met by a charitable company   16
2.5   Stationery and the legal requirements   20
2.6   Legal 'health check' and review   21
2.7   Returns to be made in accordance with the Charities Act 1993   23
2.8   Offences for which penalties are prescribed by the Charities Act 1993   24
2.9   Offences for which penalties are prescribed by companies legislation   25
2.10   Selected company forms   28
2.11   Other useful publications   28

3.   Management and organisation   35

3.1   Trustees   35
3.2   Powers of trustees   38
3.3   Duties of trustees   39
3.4   Liability of trustees   41
3.5   Transfer of title to property on retirement of a trustee   43
3.6   Honorary officers   44
3.7   Remuneration of charity trustees   46

3.8	Director/trustees of a charitable company	49
3.9	Honorary advisers	55
3.10	Employees	55
3.11	The relationship between trustees, employees and volunteers	56
3.12	Specialist advisers and consultants	60
3.13	Draft letters to be sent to a trustee or director/trustee on appointment	62
3.14	Other useful publications	64

4. Committee administration — 65

4.1	The need for committees	65
4.2	The role of the governing body	66
4.3	Terms of reference	67
4.4	Composition of committees	68

5. Governance — 70

5.1	The status, authority and liability of the secretary of a charitable company	70
5.2	Good 'boardroom practice' – a code for trustees and charity secretaries	73
5.3	Principles of good governance	74
5.4	Other useful publications	76

6. Constitutions and governing documents — 77

6.1	Incorporation – advantages and disadvantages	77
6.2	The unincorporated charity's constitution	78
6.3	The charitable company's constitution	80
6.4	Other useful publications	83

7. Meetings — 84

7.1	Frequency and timing	84
7.2	The law	85
7.3	Administration of meetings	87
7.4	Additional requirements applicable to a charitable company	90
7.5	Meetings of the members of a charitable company	91
7.6	Offences for which penalties are prescribed by companies legislation	92
7.7	Other useful publications	93

8. Property and insurance — 94

8.1	Acquisition of freehold or leasehold property	94
8.2	Funding an acquisition	97

8.3	Rating of premises owned or occupied by charities	98
8.4	Dispositions of charity land and property	98
8.5	Buildings and contents insurance	99
8.6	Other insurances	100
8.7	Insurance checklist	101
8.8	Other useful publications	102

9. Fund-raising 103

9.1	Background	103
9.2	Legacies	103
9.3	Covenants	104
9.4	Lotteries	105
9.5	Charity trading companies	106
9.6	Capital fund-raising	108
9.7	Use of consultants and professional fund-raisers	108
9.8	Checklist of provisions to be included in a fund-raising agreement	110
9.9	Precedent form of deed of covenant	112
9.10	Other useful publications	112

10. Personnel administration and employment law and practice 115

10.1	The contract of employment	115
10.2	Job security	120
10.3	Unfair dismissal	123
10.4	Health and safety at work	130
10.5	Volunteers	134
10.6	Other useful publications	135

11. Accounting and financial management 136

11.1	Financial control and compliance	136
11.2	Management accounting	139
11.3	Annual statutory accounts	142
11.4	Statutory audit or independent examination	144
11.5	Other useful publications	146

Appendices

Appendix 1	Model form of constitution of an unincorporated charitable association	147
Appendix 2	Model form of memorandum and articles of association of a charitable company	157
Appendix 3	Where to find further information	174

Index 176

INTRODUCTION

The primary purpose of this book is to help secretaries and administrators of charities and voluntary organisations carry out their role more effectively and with greater authority and certainty. The description 'secretary' is used generically and includes controller, administrator as well as all those individuals however they may be described who are responsible for the secretarial and administrative function in their organisation. For the avoidance of doubt, any reference to the masculine includes the feminine.

The range of duties carried out by charity secretaries and not-for-profit administrators is extensive and will differ in breadth and variety from one organisation to another. Apart from the relatively few charities established by Royal Charter, charities are in the main either unincorporated trusts, associations, charitable companies limited by guarantee, industrial and provident societies or friendly societies.

There are basic or core principles of practice which define the role of the secretary irrespective of the nature of the organisation. However, there are additional responsibilities as well as liabilities which attach to the secretary of a charitable company limited by guarantee because the secretary of a charitable company is an officer of the company for the purposes of the Companies Acts 1985–89.

First and foremost this book is intended to be of practical use and includes something for everyone who is connected with the administration of a charity, voluntary or not-for-profit organisation. Reference is made throughout to sources of more detailed information; for example, *The Charities Manual* also published by ICSA Publishing Ltd, various NCVO publications, and also leaflets published by the Charity Commission.

The following should be noted:

- [ ] Directors of charitable companies for the purpose of this book are called director/trustees.
- [ ] The general law relating to trustees applies equally to the trustees of an unincorporated charity as it does to the director/trustees of a charitable

company; it is just that the latter are also bound by the rules of company law and other related legislation, for example the Insolvency Act 1986.

☐ The Charities Act 1993 consolidates virtually all of the legislation governing charities. What remains of the Charities Act 1992 relates to professional fund-raising and the conduct of public appeals. Apart from exepted and exempt charities, for example universities, almost all other charities with an annual income of £1,000 or more or those owning property classified as permanent endowment must register with the Charity Commission under the 1993 Act.

Central to the role of the charity secretary is the obligation to ensure compliance – not only with the general law but also with the charity's own governing document. Chapter 6 deals specifically with constitutional matters and the procedure to be followed should it be decided to review and amend the governing document. Model draft constitutions for an unincorporated charitable association and a charitable company are set out in Appendices 1 and 2. Reference to specific clauses in the appendices is made where appropriate. There is also the question of how the principles of 'good governance' should be upheld and the extent to which it is (or should be) the secretary's duty to maintain appropriate standards. Consequently this issue is dealt with specifically in Chapter 5.

It hardly needs to be said that the role of the charity secretary is a very worthwhile and rewarding one – if not always in monetary terms. Nonetheless some will be concerned about the implications and exactly what it is that they may be taking on. This is particularly so if the secretary is a volunteer and doing the job purely for altruistic or personal reasons.

Although this book deals primarily with the essentials of the charity secretary's responsibilities it is also intended to be sufficiently comprehensive to help guide secretaries and administrators through what at times must seem to be a legal and administrative minefield – or perhaps a 'quagmire' may be the more accurate description. It is hoped that this book will also be of general interest and use to those who advise on charity matters, principally solicitors and accountants.

My grateful thanks to Caroline Knight for producing a number of drafts of the typescript and for making order out of my chaos. I am grateful also to David Prescott for a number of suggestions which I have included. Any errors which remain are my responsibility alone.

References to the law are believed to be accurate as at February 1998.

Malcolm Leatherdale

1

THE ROLE AND CORE DUTIES OF THE CHARITY SECRETARY

1.1 The need for competent administration

Performance monitoring

Any charitable organisation, even the smallest, should not only adopt appropriate administrative procedures but also provide the means and the will to monitor performance and to adapt and improve the procedures as necessary.

Establishing a sound administrative system is an investment well worth making, because an efficient charity effectively run inspires confidence not only among supporters and fund-raisers, but volunteers and beneficiaries as well; it is also more likely that the charity will attain its objects. In addition morale among any staff employed by the larger charity should be enhanced.

Good or best practice

In many respects the role of the secretary of an unincorporated charity or one established by Royal Charter is the same as that of the secretary of a charitable company limited by guarantee and not having a share capital; the principles of good practice apply equally. Good or best practice, for example in the organisation, administration and conduct of meetings, the maintenance of financial records, the promotion of good communication, the preparation and consideration of timely financial data, and the arrangement of appropriate insurance cover are essential to the well-being of all charities however they are constituted as well as other organisations in the not-for-profit sector.

Requirements of company law

The secretary of a charitable company must also ensure that it complies with the requirements of company law.

Just because a charitable company has a charitable purpose does not mean it is exempt from the obligations imposed by company law – for example if a company is more than twelve months late in filing its annual accounts with the Registrar of Companies the penalty to be paid may be as much as £1,000.

1.2 The role of the secretary

Extent

The extent of the jobholder's duties and responsibilities (and influence) will vary depending on the nature of the organisation, for example:

- ☐ The secretary may be the chief administrative officer acting in tandem with a chief executive. In addition to being the chief administrative officer the secretary may also have specific or departmental management responsibilities and in some cases may have a great deal of influence over the direction of the charity acting with the support of the trustees. The extent to which this happens varies in practice because responsibilities become blurred and overlapping. Consequently there is the need to draw clear lines of demarcation between the secretary, the chief executive and the trustees. The fundamental principle is that trustees set the policy for the charity and the management carry out and implement that policy, although in practice the formulation of policy is often the product of the executive staff and the trustees working together for the benefit of the charity.
- ☐ Alternatively the secretary may be someone who carries out a purely administrative function dealing with correspondence, the servicing of meetings and perhaps maintaining the accounts with very little influence or involvement in any other area of the charity's activity.
- ☐ At the other end of the spectrum the secretary may also be the chief executive with controlling and management responsibilities either with administrative responsibilities (which is more likely) or not. Again such a secretary may have as much influence as the trustees.

Size and constitution of the charity

It can be seen therefore that the role will vary considerably from one charity to another. It will also be determined partly by the size and constitution of the charity and partly by the personality and character of the secretary in relation to the chief executive, if the secretary is not also the chief executive, and of course the personalities and characters of the trustees.

The role of the secretary will also depend to some extent on the objectives of the charity and it should therefore be appreciated that there is no 'identi-kit' for the charity secretary, although there are some general similarities which are shared by all secretaries and administrators of charities, voluntary and not-for-profit organisations.

1.3   The core duties and responsibilities of the secretary

Providing general and administrative support to the trustees

A core function of the secretary is to ensure that any correspondence which is generated as a result of decisions made by the trustees is dealt with promptly and efficiently. The relationship of the secretary to the trustees or to an individual trustee of any charity will as already mentioned vary like much else according to the size and type of the organisation and the personalities of those concerned. It will also depend on the level of involvement of each trustee and how available they are on a day-to-day basis.

The secretary should be clear as to the respective roles of the trustees on the one hand and those who carry out administration and day-to-day management on the other. Trustees will usually look to the secretary for information and advice on all aspects which relate to the charity and of which they do not have direct knowledge or experience themselves.

Ideally the secretary should organise an induction programme for any new trustee and in the course of such a programme should:

- ☐ explain the purposes and objects of the charity and its status;
- ☐ provide a copy of the charity's governing document or memorandum and articles of association in the case of a charitable company with a summary of the more important provisions;
- ☐ arrange a meeting with the other trustees to enable the new trustee to discuss with them how they are fulfilling their charity's purpose and objects;
- ☐ explain the terms of any personal liability insurance cover there may be;
- ☐ provide a copy of the latest set of accounts or financial statements with an explanation of the figures; and
- ☐ provide a copy of the strategic plan (if any) and a current financial forecast.

It should also be clear to whom the secretary reports on certain matters and this again will to some extent depend on the size and complexity of the organisation and the nature of the charity's field of activity. Some charities are very bureaucratic in the way they are organised, although conversely in the case of many charities it is administrative and organisational constraints that prevent new opportunities from being developed apart from any lack of funding.

Arrangement and administration of meetings of the governing body

A prime responsibility of the secretary is to organise the meetings of the governing body, any committees and sub-committees, and to prepare and circulate notices of such meetings. Subsequent to each meeting the minutes must be drafted, approved and circulated. How widely the draft minutes should be circulated is debatable. It is for each secretary in conjunction with the chairman to decide an appropriate procedure which will vary from one organisation to another.

Acting as the point of communication both internally and externally

The secretary will provide the means by which communication takes place both internally and externally. The secretary must therefore institute effective systems and procedures for ensuring good communication upwards, downwards and across the organisation. Unless the charity employs its own media/communications manager the secretary will usually be the point of contact between the charity and those who have dealings with it, including the media, governmental agencies, professional advisers, as well as the trustees and beneficiaries.

Communicating and implementing the decisions and instructions of the trustees

The role of the secretary in fulfilling this requirement will like much else depend on the size and scope of the organisation. The secretary of a small charity comprising relatively few individuals and where the chain of communication is short will have a different degree of involvement and responsibility than would for example the secretary of a charity with several hundred employees and a large number of volunteers. One useful practice in achieving better communication would be to circulate the minutes of the meetings of any sub-committees to the trustees as a whole.

Communicating with the members and supporters of the charity

This is most important. The secretary is the point of contact between the charity and its trustees on the one hand and the members and supporters of the charity on the other. It should also be noted that members and supporters may not necessarily be the same people because not all supporters are members in the technical sense – see clauses 4/6 of Appendix 1 and clauses 3/5 of Appendix 2.

It may be difficult at times to identify precisely those individuals who are the members and who ultimately have control of the charity. In the case of a charitable company the register of members must be kept up to date, and if this is done there should be no difficulty in identifying the members and circulating them with a copy of the annual report and accounts each year and notices of general meetings, either annual or extraordinary. Failure to maintain the register of members would constitute a breach of s. 352 of the Companies Act 1985.

It may be more of a problem in the case of an unincorporated charitable association to identify who are the members and therefore entitled to attend and vote at general meetings. The main principle to follow, as already mentioned, is to be sure that the definition of who is a member is clear and that the membership records are also accurate and up to date.

Arranging annual or extraordinary general meetings of the members of the charity

The secretary is responsible for preparing and circulating notices of general meetings to the members of a charity and preparing the minutes in conjunction with the chairman of the meeting.

Legal guidance and advice

The secretary should preferably have more than just a working knowledge of charity law as well as some knowledge of the basics of company legislation if he is the secretary of a charitable company. The more the secretary is proficient in these areas the less it will cost the charity in legal and accountancy fees although Charity Commission and Companies House personnel are usually helpful in providing assistance and advice. The secretary also ought to have a fairly detailed knowledge of the legislation which affects his particular charity, for example residential home legislation where the charity operates such homes or the Control of Substances Hazardous to Health Regulations 1994 for those organisations which have research laboratories. It is also important for the secretary to understand the fundamentals of the law and practice of employment and in particular health and safety legislation. This is dealt with in more detail in Chapter 10.

Additionally, some experience in vetting contracts is another useful skill to acquire particularly in what has become known euphemistically as the 'contract culture'.

Compliance with statutory and other regulatory requirements

The secretary must ensure that all formal returns prescribed by charities and companies legislation are submitted to the Charity Commission or the Registrar of Companies respectively and that the requisite statutory registers and records are also maintained. The secretary of a charitable company must in particular ensure the maintenance of the register of members, the register of director/trustees, the minute books for meetings of director/trustees and of any committees as well as the general meetings of the members of a charitable company as required by companies legislation.

Conversely, there are no statutory obligations regarding the keeping of minutes of the meetings of an unincorporated charity but if the charity has a governing document (and unfortunately not every charity does) there is usually a requirement to that effect.

Co-ordination

The various elements which constitute a charity's activity and purpose need to be co-ordinated and the secretary is well placed to take a leading role in helping to achieve this.

Acting as the conscience of the charity

To some extent the secretary also acts as the conscience of the charity, although he should not be expected to do so too often! The secretary must act with integrity and with a degree of independence in order to protect the interests of the charity, its trustees, its members, beneficiaries, supporters, and staff if any. It is also important that the secretary should maintain at all times a thoroughly professional approach to the way in which he performs the role and discharges his responsibilities. This applies equally to the secretary of a charity as it does to any organisation in the not-for-profit sector. It also has a bearing on the way in which appropriate standards of governance are formulated and maintained by a charity, a topic which is discussed in more detail in Chapter 5.

Acting as the custodian of the charity's governing document

The secretary also acts as the custodian of the charity's governing document whether it is a trust deed or memorandum and articles of association. Consequently the secretary must ensure that the charity keeps within the parameters of its governing document. The governing document should be reviewed by the secretary from time to time in conjunction with the trustees and where necessary changes to the governing document should be instituted.

Property and insurance

The extent and responsibility will vary. In many cases the secretary will have little or no involvement because the charity has no premises of its own, and insurance generally is a minor matter, in terms of time, although very important in practice. This topic is dealt with in more detail in Chapter 8.

Fund-raising

Many charity secretaries will be involved in fund-raising. The secretary of a larger charity will usually have some responsibility although how much will depend on whether or not the charity employs its own fund-raising personnel and department. This topic is dealt with more fully in Chapter 9 which also includes a discussion of the basic elements of an agreement between a charity and a professional fund-raiser.

Personnel administration and practice

The secretary will usually be responsible to some extent for personnel matters if the charity is an employer, although the involvement will be limited if the charity itself employs a personnel officer. However, the secretary should be aware of the legal status of volunteers compared with employed staff, and the way in which (when circumstances require) the correct dismissal procedure should be followed, topics which feature in Chapter 10.

Accounting and taxation

Again it will depend on the nature of the charity as to the secretary's responsibility for accounting and taxation matters. Smaller charities usually appoint an honorary treasurer and larger charities will employ their own accounting personnel. The secretary will however have some involvement arising out of his responsibility for preparing meetings of the trustees and may also from time to time, for example corresponding with the auditors. This topic is dealt with in more detail in Chapter 11.

Dealing with the bank

The secretary will often be the person who corresponds with the charity's bank and will also be a party to any negotiations with the bank in conjunction with the charity's own financial personnel.

Anything else!

Anything which does not fit into a particular category or for which no one else will or can take responsibility usually falls to the secretary to do. One example would be to be appointed as the director/secretary of a subsidiary trading company although the scope is endless.

2

COMPLIANCE AND THE LAW

2.1 General compliance

The Charities Act 1993

Charity trustees have to comply with an increasing amount of legislation in addition to the common or general trust law by which they are also governed. The secretary should be aware of the main requirements of the Charities Act 1993 and keep up to date with its implementation and any court or Charity Commission decisions so that he can give proper advice to the trustees as questions arise and circumstances require.

Voluntary work for a charity can be interesting and rewarding, but the obligations which trustees take on have become increasingly onerous, and even more so for the trustee who is a director/trustee of a charitable company. Nor is a charity trustee entitled to receive payment other than reimbursement of out-of-pocket expenses except in particular circumstances – unlike the director of a commercial company. The Charity Commission leaflet which deals with this subject is CC11.

Trustees have acquired additional responsibilities by virtue of the 1993 Act. There is also the risk that they can be made personally liable if they are in breach of the law. A number of the provisions of the 1993 Act reinforce some of the principles of trust law, for example the trustees' general duty of care. Apart from financial penalties which may be levied there is also the possibility that a charity trustee may be disqualified from continuing to act.

Accountability of trustees

The role of the charity trustee has never been short of responsibility. It can require a considerable expenditure of time and application; it also requires an understanding of the legal and other obligations which arise. Most trustees are unaware that they incur the risk of personal liability to third parties in respect of any commitment they enter into on behalf of their charity (except in the case of a director/trustee acting on behalf of a charitable company where the principle of limited liability applies). In some respects trustees who contract on behalf of their charity are in the same position as if they had given a personal guarantee. This topic is dealt with in more detail in Chapter 3.

Supervisory role of the Charity Commission

The 1993 Act provides a framework for the more effective management and public accountability of charities and their trustees. Part of the intention behind the new legislation was to introduce a system which would enable the Charity Commission to invest more resources in its supervisory role which had not been carried out as rigorously in the past as it perhaps should have been. The 1993 Act transfers many of the administrative duties previously exercised by the Commission directly to charity trustees. This new regime is intended to give more freedom to charities to control their own affairs although the net result is that trustees will now have to demonstrate a greater duty of general care and responsibility than before and perhaps pay a price if they fail to do so!

2.2   Compliance with charities legislation

Requirement that charity changes its name

The Charity Commission now has the power to direct any registered charity including a charitable company to change its name within a specified period to another name which the trustees may choose but which also may have to be approved by the Commission. The grounds on which the Commission can order the name of a charity to be changed are:

- ☐ that it is the same as that of another registered charity; or
- ☐ is in the opinion of the Commission too similar to such a name; or
- ☐ that the name is likely to mislead the public; or
- ☐ that the name may give the impression that the charity is connected with the government or a local authority; or
- ☐ is in the opinion of the Commission offensive.

Where such a direction is given in the case of a charitable company its effect is to require the name of the company to be changed by a resolution of the director/trustees of the company – it does not require a resolution of the members of the company as would be the case if the company had decided to change its name of its own volition.

Power of Charity Commission to institute inquiries

The Charity Commission has power under the 1993 Act to institute inquiries regarding charities generally or a particular charity. These powers are very wide-ranging and include the power to order the production of accounts and statements in writing in regard to any matter which is being investigated. The Commission can require evidence to be taken on oath and may publish a report of its findings. The Commission may also require any person to provide it with information which they have in their possession and which relates to the charity under investigation. Such a person would clearly include the secretary and it is also worth noting that it is an offence to suppress, conceal, or destroy relevant documents and that anyone who is guilty of such an offence is liable to a fine or a term of imprisonment not exceeding two years or both.

Dealing with land

Until the passage of the 1992 Charities Act a charity which wanted to dispose of land had to obtain the consent of the Charity Commission before doing so. The relevant provisions in the 1992 Act were re-enacted by the 1993 Act. The trustees of charities selling land or buildings except on rare occasions will no longer have to obtain the formal consent of the Commission provided they follow the prescribed statutory procedures. These are not burdensome or complicated and are set out in more detail in Chapter 8.

Accounting records

Charity trustees must ensure that accurate accounting records are kept which are sufficient to show and explain all of the charity's financial transactions. The records must be retained for six years from the end of the charity's financial year to which they relate, which overrides the requirement in the case of a charitable company that the financial records need only be retained for three years.

Annual accounting statements

Charity trustees have to prepare in respect of each financial year of their charity accounting statements which comply with the requirements prescribed by regulations made by the Secretary of State – these came into effect on 1 March 1996. The regulations, together with the Statement of Recommended Practice – the Charities SORP – constitute the new accounting framework for charities which also includes charitable companies. The new accounting regime for charities is contained in the Charity Commission's leaflets CC51/56.

Copies of accounts to be made available on request

One requirement which emphasises public accountability and with which every charity has to comply regardless of its size, or how it is constituted, is to provide members of the public with a copy of its most recent accounts on request. Any audit or independent examination report must also be attached to the accounts provided in response to such a request. The trustees must comply with any such request within two months and if they fail to do so they will be liable to a fine on conviction.

Audit

The 1993 Act provides that if a charity's level of income or expenditure reaches particular thresholds it will be obliged to have its accounts either audited or independently examined, although there are some complications with regard to charitable companies where separate rules prescribed by the Companies Act 1985 also apply. The Charities (Accounts and Reports) Regulations 1995 are considered further in Chapter 11.

Filing of annual accounts

The statutory annual accounts of a charity (audited or independently examined where necessary) must be sent with its annual report to the Charity Commission within ten months of the financial year end of the charity where its income or expenditure exceeds £10,000 in the year concerned. Charities below the £10,000 threshold do not have to send their annual accounts to the Commission unless specifically requested to do so by the Commission.

Annual reports

The 1993 Act obliges all charity trustees to prepare in respect of each financial year of their charity an annual report the nature of which partly depends on the level of annual income or expenditure of the individual charity. In the case of a charity which has neither income nor expenditure above £10,000 the annual report only has to be sent to the Charity Commission if requested. Otherwise the annual report of the charity together with its statement of accounts must be sent to the Commission within ten months of the end of the financial year of the charity or within such longer period as the Commission may for any special reason allow. Any person who is persistently in default of this requirement will be liable to a fine on conviction. See also sections 2.7 and 11.3.

2.3 Compliance with companies legislation

Routine obligations

The obligations placed on the director/trustees of a charitable company are contained in general company law and more particularly in the Companies Acts 1985–89. Charitable companies are obliged to:

- Maintain a register of members.
- Maintain a register of director/trustees and secretaries.
- Maintain adequate accounting records.
- Maintain minute books containing the minutes of the meetings of director/trustees *and* of the members.
- Maintain a register of charges and mortgages (if any).
- Notify the Registrar of any changes in the particulars of director/trustees or secretaries and of their appointment or resignation.
- Prepare an annual return to be sent to the Registrar – this requirement does *not* depend on any specific financial threshold.

These matters are dealt with in more detail in section 2.4.

Extent to which companies legislation applies

Many of the provisions of companies legislation apply equally to charitable companies limited by guarantee as they do to large international companies listed on the Stock Exchange. There are of course many additional regulations affecting public companies which are listed, but much of company law is common to all companies however constituted.

Elective regime

Some company law provisions relate specifically to private companies, for example the elective regime introduced by the Companies Act 1989. The elective regime enables a private company to convene a general meeting to pass various resolutions termed elective resolutions so it can, for example, dispense with the obligation to present annual accounts and reports to a general meeting of the members, or the requirement to hold an annual general meeting or to appoint auditors annually.

The elective regime is more beneficial to a private trading company where the owners are also the managers; it is not particularly appropriate for use by a charitable company where it is important that the periodic involvement of the members who are usually its supporters and fund-raisers should be retained and indeed encouraged.

2.4   Additional requirements to be met by a charitable company

Maintenance and inspection of statutory registers and books

The Companies Act 1985 provides that any register, index, minute book or accounting records required by the 1985 Act to be maintained by *all* companies can be kept either by making the entries in a bound book or by recording such information in any other appropriate manner. If the entries are not made in a bound book (the probable alternative would be loose-leaf) adequate security precautions must be taken to guard against falsification. A fine can be imposed in the event of default.

The 1985 Act specifies the information to be included in each record and register which has to be kept, as well as where such records and registers are to be located and the rights of inspection. The Secretary of State has the power to make regulations regarding the obligation of companies to allow inspection of their registers, and to specify how much can be charged for providing copies of the information recorded. The rates are very modest.

The right to require copies of the entries in the register is now governed by the Companies (Inspection and Copying of Registers, Indices and Documents) Regulations 1991.

Register of members

The register must contain the names and addresses of all the company's members and where there are more than fifty members an index is also required unless the register is in such a form which automatically constitutes an index, for example if the members are listed in alphabetical order.

The register must be kept at the registered office of the company unless it is maintained elsewhere. It may for example be kept at the office of the charitable company's auditors or at the 'place of business' of the company which may not necessarily be its registered office. Notification must be sent to the Registrar of Companies if the register is kept other than at the registered office. The register and any index normally has to be open for inspection by any member of the charitable company without charge and any other person on payment of the prescribed fee which is £2.50 for each hour or part of an hour, or a lesser charge if appropriate for not less than two hours each business day between 9 a.m. and 5 p.m.

In addition a member or any other person can request copies of the register and any index or any part on payment of the prescribed fee which is £2.50 for the first 100 entries, £20.00 for the next 1,000 entries and £15.00 for every subsequent 1,000 entries or such lesser sum as may be agreed. The company has ten days within which to comply with a request for copies of the entries in the register. If there is default in complying with these provisions then the company and every officer who is in default is liable to a fine and for continued contravention a daily default fine.

Register of director/trustees and secretaries

A charitable company must maintain a register of director/trustees and secretaries recording the specified information for each individual.

In the case of the director/trustees there has to be recorded for each one their date of birth, present forenames and surnames, and any other names changed since the age of eighteen if used within the last twenty years. However the maiden name or any previous married names of a female do not need to be shown. The register must also disclose the usual residential (not business) address of each director/trustee, his nationality and business occupation if any. Particulars of other current directorships and past directorships held within the previous five years must also be included.

The information to be recorded in respect of the secretary must include his full name, surname and usual residential address. The rules relating to former names are the same as those which apply to a director/trustee but there is no requirement that the date of birth of the secretary should be stated or details of any directorships held.

The register of director/trustees and secretaries must be kept at the registered office of the charitable company and be open for inspection by the members of the company without charge and by any other person on the same basis as mentioned on page 16 above. If an inspection is refused the company and every officer who is in default is liable to a fine.

As a charitable company is limited by guarantee there are no shares and consequently there is no need to maintain a register of directors' interests in shares.

Notification of changes

Where a new director/trustee or secretary is appointed, form 288a has to be completed and signed by the director/trustee or secretary as the case may be, and countersigned by an existing director/trustee or secretary, before it is sent to the Registrar.

Any changes to the respective particulars of the director/trustees of a charitable company or the secretary recorded in the register must be notified to the Registrar on form 288c within fourteen days of their occurrence. It is important that the up-to-date forms are used which can be obtained either from a law stationer or the Registrar of Companies. If a director/trustee or secretary is removed or resigns form 288b must be completed and signed by a continuing director/trustee or secretary and sent to the Registrar.

Accounting records

The 1985 Companies Act specifies the requirements to be met by companies in regard to the keeping of accounting records. Such records are treated as statutory records, and failure to maintain them will render any officer (which includes the secretary) who is in default guilty of an offence unless he can show that he acted honestly and in all the circumstances should be excused from blame.

The 1985 Act also states that a private company must preserve its accounting records for three years from the date on which they were made. Again, failure to do so will render an officer of the company liable to court proceedings which could result in imprisonment or a fine or both. The accounting records may be kept elsewhere than at the company's registered office if the director/trustees so decide but must be available for inspection by the officers of the company at all times. If, however, the charitable company is a registered charity it will have to keep its accounting records for six years as already mentioned.

Minute books

The 1985 Act requires that minutes are kept of the meetings of director/trustees as well as general meetings of the members of any company, charitable or otherwise. It is also a requirement that the minutes of proceedings at general meetings be kept at the registered office of the company and be open to inspection by any member for at least two hours between 9 a.m. and 5 p.m. on each business day. The refusal to allow an inspection would render the company and any officer in default liable to a fine and if the refusal continues a further fine may be imposed. Members of a charitable company are also entitled to receive copies of the minutes of any general meetings of the company within seven days of the request being made. The company is entitled to charge 10 pence for each 100 words copied.

Minutes of the meetings of director/trustees are not, however, required to be available for inspection as these are confidential. It is therefore sensible to keep separate books for the minutes of general meetings of a charitable company and the minutes of meetings of the director/trustees and any committees.

Register of charges and mortgages

Every company is obliged by the 1985 Act as amended by the 1989 Act, to keep at its registered office a register of charges and mortgages even if there are no entries to be made because no charges or mortgages have been created. The register must contain details of all charges or mortgages specifically affecting any property of the charitable company and all floating charges over the company's assets. Each entry must include a short description of the property charged or mortgaged, the principal amount of the charge or mortgage, and the name of the person or company which is entitled to enforce the charge or mortgage.

A company must also keep a copy of any instrument creating a charge or mortgage required to be registered with the Registrar. Such copy instruments, together with the company's register of charges and mortgages, must be available for inspection by any creditor or member without payment and to any other person on payment of not more than 5 pence for each inspection for at least two hours between 9 a.m. and 5 p.m. on each business day. There are penalties for refusing an inspection.

It is also mandatory that the company sends particulars to the Registrar of any charges or mortgages created using the prescribed form within twenty-one days of the creation of the charge or mortgage as the case may be. If the company fails to do so the company and every officer in default is liable to a fine. In practice what usually happens is that the lender or lender's solicitors will arrange to notify the Registrar within the twenty-one-day period, as another consequence of the failure to do so would be to render the charge void against a liquidator in the event that the company went into insolvent liquidation.

Circulation of the statutory accounts and reports

The 1989 Act provides that at least twenty-one days before the date of the general meeting at which the statutory accounts and respective reports of the auditors and director/trustees are to be presented to the members of the company (which is normally the annual general meeting) a copy of those documents must be sent to every member and to every other person who is entitled under the 1989 Act to receive such copies. The twenty-one days' notice required are clear days, which means that the day on which the notice is deemed to be given and the day of the meeting itself do not count. The articles of association usually provide that any notice is deemed to be given at the expiration of a specified period, for example forty-eight hours after the envelope containing the notice was posted.

Annual return

The annual return is issued by the Registrar and based on information filed at Companies House. It is sent to the company for checking, amendment if necessary, signature by a director/trustee or the secretary and return to the Registrar.

There are specific rules regarding the date to which the annual return has to be made up. It must be submitted to Companies House by reference to a return date which is the anniversary of the company's incorporation, or if the company's last delivered annual return was made up to a different date, the anniversary of that date. The current requirement for delivering the annual return to the Registrar is that it must be done within twenty-eight days of the return date. A filing fee is also payable. Failure to file an annual return may lead to the prosecution of an officer of the company.

2.5 Stationery and the legal requirements

Obligation to state that charity is registered on certain publications

Every registered charity (including a charitable company) which in its last financial year had a gross income in excess of £10,000 (formerly £5,000) is obliged to state in English the fact that it is a registered charity on all notices, advertisements, appeals for funds, and on other official documents including bills of exchange, promissory notes, cheques and orders for money or goods, invoices, receipts and letters of credit. It is not, as is often believed, obligatory for the charity's registered number to appear on its documents but it is a common practice nonetheless. It is a punishable offence for any person, including a trustee or the secretary, to authorise the issue of a document which does not comply with these requirements.

Additional requirements to be met by a charitable company

The stationery and various other documents issued by or on behalf of a charitable company must comply with a number of additional requirements which are contained in the Companies Act 1985 and the Charities Act 1993. These requirements are less than straightforward but failure to comply constitutes an offence.

A director/trustee, employee or officer of a charitable company (the treasurer or secretary for example) who authorises the issue of specified documents which do not comply with the legal requirements can be personally liable, although the court may excuse an officer (which would include a director/trustee, treasurer or secretary) from liability if there is sufficient reason to do so.

The 1985 Act provides that every company (which includes a charitable company) must have its *name* mentioned in legible characters on the following:

☐ All business letters.
☐ All notices and other official publications.
☐ All bills of exchange, promissory notes, endorsements, cheques and orders for money or goods purporting to be signed by or on behalf of the company.

- [ ] All invoices, receipts and letters of credit.

Where the name of the charitable company does not include the word 'charity' or 'charitable' the fact that it is a charity must be stated in legible characters on all the items mentioned above and in addition a conveyance (which means any instrument creating, transferring, varying or extinguishing an interest in land) entered into by a charitable company must include a statement that it is a charity or is charitable.

The 1985 Act also requires that the following *particulars* must be mentioned in legible characters on all *business letters* and *order forms* issued by a charitable company:

- [ ] The company's place of registration, i.e. England and Wales.
- [ ] Its registered company number.
- [ ] Its registered office address.
- [ ] In the case of a company exempt from the obligation to use the word 'limited' as part of its name the fact that it is a limited company.

Although it is a legal requirement that the registered number of every company must be stated on its letterhead it is not obligatory as mentioned on page 20 above that its registered charity number should also be stated. However, in practice most charitable companies (confusingly) do so. The only obligations in this respect are to include a statement that the charitable company is a charity and that if it is registered that it is a registered charity.

It is not obligatory to state on the letterhead of a charitable company the names of the director/trustees but if it is decided to do so then all the director/trustees must be named and not just some. Any employee whose name appears on a charitable company's letterhead must be correctly designated to ensure that he is not held out as a director/trustee. Someone who is not a director/trustee (and sometimes the distinction is blurred) but who has a 'figurehead' appointment should be designated by their title, for example president, or patron, and clearly separated from where the names of the director/trustees appear.

The problem that can easily arise is for the letterhead of a charitable company to become too cluttered with telephone and fax numbers as well as both registered numbers. Care should therefore be taken to avoid any such confusion and thoughtful design is well worth the effort. There is a model draft letterhead (with variations) for a charitable company on page 29.

2.6 Legal 'health check' and review

Legal audit

The secretary should from time to time consider a number of matters as part of the legal audit of his charity's 'modus operandi'. Some of the topics in this section appear elsewhere but drawing the main elements together in one place is intended as a convenient *aide-mémoire*. The following are suggested but are not in any order of priority.

Governing document

The contents of the trust deed, constitution or memorandum and articles of association of a charitable company as the case may be should be reviewed from time to time to ensure that the provisions are appropriate to the current management and operation of the charity or charitable company.

Freehold and leasehold property

The procedures which are adopted when freehold premises are being acquired or sold or when leases are being acquired assigned or terminated should be reviewed. The basis on which negotiations are carried out and by whom and whether there should be terms of reference or guidance for general issue should be considered, as should the arrangements for the storage of deeds. Is there a proper index system in place? Check also how documents of title to freehold or leasehold property should be executed by the charity and in the case of a charitable company consider whether or not it is appropriate to dispense with the common seal.

Employment and personnel procedures

Consider the procedures relating to the employment of staff and in particular how letters of offer are drafted, their content and the format of contracts (or written statement of the main terms) of employment. Check and review for example the adequacy of grievance and disciplinary procedures and that the legal requirements to provide equal opportunities are being met.

Charities and companies legislation and general trust law

Review what guidance is given to a trustee on appointment and subsequently in order to keep him up to date. Review the management, organisation and the procedures adopted for the meetings of trustees or director/trustees. Check that such meetings are properly constituted and whether there are any shortcomings which could lead to a breach of procedure or trust.

Health and safety legislation

Consider whether there are adequate procedures in place and how any changes in the law are monitored so that there is due compliance with UK and also EU law in a way which is proactive rather than reactive. Ensure that a written safety policy is devised and published if the charity has more than five employees.

Contracts and terms and conditions

Review the procedures for entering into contracts for the purchase of commodities and services. Review and bring up to date general or standard terms and conditions of purchase if there are any and where appropriate standardise procedures. Review any equipment hire agreements or finance leases, in particular those relating to photocopiers.

Contested legacies and delays in payment

Review the way in which correspondence is conducted with solicitors acting on behalf of the executors of estates where the charity is a beneficiary. In particular consider what approach should be taken where there is undue delay before a legacy is received or payment made on account.

Other legislation

Consider compliance procedures relating to lotteries legislation and the legal implications of other fund-raising activities, for example the holding of open-air events. Review or introduce procedures which should be in place to deal with local authorities where the grant of an entertainments licence is required. Substantial payments may be levied by some local authorities for the grant of such a licence and therefore consideration should be given to ways in which such costs can be kept to a minimum. A system should be established to monitor developments in the law which affect the charity and its purpose.

Trading activities

Review the basis on which the charity trades or may be intending to trade through a subsidiary trading company.

2.7 Returns to be made in accordance with the Charities Act 1993

Annual return

Part VI of the 1993 Act came into effect on 1 March 1996. Every registered charity (including a charitable company) whose annual gross income or total expenditure exceeds £10,000 is required to prepare in respect of each of its financial years an annual return in such form and containing such information as may be required by any regulations made by the Charity Commission. Annual returns are part of the means by which the Commission can fulfil its responsibility to supervise charities in order that public confidence in the sector can be maintained and enhanced. The submission of annual returns will also help the Commission to discharge its wider monitoring obligations. Some of the questions are framed in such a way that the answers should enable the Commission to identify possible causes for concern in the administration of charities.

The annual return will be sent by the Commission to those individuals nominated for correspondence, for completion. That individual will usually be the secretary. The annual return, together with the annual report to which the accounts are to be attached, must as already mentioned be submitted within ten months of the end of the relevant financial year if the income or expenditure of the charity exceeds £10,000.

Monitoring

The monitoring of charities by the Commission will ensure that charities are given help and advice when potential problems or difficulties arise. The main way in which this is intended to be achieved is through analysis of the statutory annual returns, accounts information and any issues which arise from the annual reports of charity trustees.

Charity Commission database

The Commission is continuing to compile a database containing all records and details of registered charities. The central register of charities is available on the internet.

2.8   Offences for which penalties are prescribed by the Charities Act 1993

The relevant section of the Act is stated in the margin.

- 5(4)   The failure to show on documents issued by the charity the fact that it is a registered charity.
- 11(3)   The supply by any person knowingly or recklessly of false or misleading information to the Commission.
- 18(14)   Contravention of an order made by the Commission following an inquiry confirming misconduct or mismanagement in the

COMPLIANCE AND THE LAW • 25

	administration of a charity or a decision taken to protect the property of a charity.
49	Persistent default in relation to the preparation and submission of an annual report to the Commission, the provision of a copy of the most recent accounts to any person requesting a copy and the transmission of an annual return to the Commission.
64	The failure to deliver to the Registrar a printed copy of a charitable company's altered memorandum and articles of association.
68	The failure by a charitable company to show on business letters, etc. that it is a charity.
73	Acting as a charity trustee while disqualified.

2.9 Offences for which penalties are prescribed by companies legislation

The relevant section of the Companies Act 1985 as amended by the Companies Act 1989 is stated in the margin. The list is not exhaustive but comprises the offences more relevant to a charitable company limited by guarantee.

Memorandum and articles of association

6(3)	The failure to deliver to the Registrar a notice or other document following alteration of a company's objects.
18(3)	The failure to register any alteration in the memorandum or articles.
19(2)	The failure to send to a member a copy of the memorandum or articles, when so requested.
20(2)	Where the memorandum is altered, issuing a copy without the alteration.
31(5)	Altering the memorandum or articles so that the company ceases to be exempt from having 'limited' as part of the company's name.
380(5)	The failure to send copies of certain resolutions to the Registrar.
380(6)	The failure to include a copy of a resolution (to which this section applies) with every copy of the articles subsequently issued, or to forward a copy of any such resolution to a member on request.

General compliance

28(5)	The failure to change the name of a company on the direction of the Secretary of State.
31(6)	The failure to change the name of a company on the direction of the Secretary of State so as to include 'limited' (or Welsh equivalent) at the end.

32(4)   The failure to change the name of a company on the direction of the Secretary of State because the name is misleading.
305(3)   Default in complying with the requirement that directors' names must appear on company correspondence, etc.
349(3)   Officer issuing business letter or document not bearing the company's name.
349(4)   Officer signing cheque, bill of exchange, etc. on which the company's name is not included.
351(5)(b) Officer or agent issuing, or authorising, the issue of a business document which does not comply.
351(5)(c) Default in complying with the requirement that information in English be stated on Welsh company's business correspondence, etc.
389A(2) Officer making a false, misleading or deceptive statement to the auditors.
394A(4) The failure to comply with the requirements as to a statement by a person ceasing to hold office as auditor.
410(4)   The failure to comply with the regulations (crystallisation of charges).
447(6)   The failure to comply with any requirements imposed by the Secretary of State to produce books and papers.
449(2)   Wrongful disclosure of information or documents obtained under s. 447 or s. 448.
450   Destroying or mutilating company documents; falsifying documents or making false entries; parting with documents or altering them or making omissions.
451   Making a false statement or explanation in purported compliance with s. 447.
458   Being a party to the carrying on of business with intent to defraud creditors, or for any fraudulent purpose.

Statutory registers and keeping of minutes

288(4)   Default in complying with the requirement to keep a register of directors and secretaries and refusal of inspection.
352(5)   Default in complying with the requirement to keep a register of members and their particulars.
382(5)   Default in complying with the requirement to keep minutes of all proceedings of general meetings and meetings of directors.
383(4)   The refusal to allow the inspection of minutes of general meetings; failure to send copies of minutes to a member on request.
411(4)   The failure to keep copies of charging instruments or register at registered office.

COMPLIANCE AND THE LAW • 27

412(4) Refusing inspection of charging instruments or register or failing to supply copies.
722(3) The failure to keep registers, minute books and accounting records in the manner required.

Statutory returns

363(3) The failure to submit an annual return to the Registrar.
387(2) The failure to give the Secretary of State notice of the non-appointment of auditors.
391(2) The failure to give notice to the Registrar of the removal of an auditor.

Report and accounts

221(5) and
222(4) The failure to keep accounting records (liability of officers).
222(6) Officer failing to secure compliance with the requirement to preserve accounting records for the requisite number of years.
233(6) Laying or delivering of unsigned balance sheet or circulating copies of a balance sheet unsigned.
234A(4) Laying, circulating or delivering a directors' report unsigned.
236(4) Laying, circulating or delivering an auditors' report unsigned.
238(5) The failure to send annual accounts, directors' report and auditors' report to those entitled to receive them.
239(3) The failure to supply a copy of accounts and reports to a member on demand.
240(6) The failure to comply with the requirements concerning publication of accounts.

Registered office

287(3) The failure to have a registered office or the failure to notify the Registrar of a change in its situation.
348(2) The failure to paint or affix name outside place of business and failure to keep painted or affixed.

Company seal

350(2) Officer using company seal without company's name engraved on it.

2.10 Selected company forms

See pages 30–4.

2.11 Other useful publications

Cairns, E. *Charities: Law and Practice* (1997) Sweet & Maxwell.
Picarda, H. *The Law and Practice Relating to Charities* (1996) Butterworth.
The Charities Manual (loose-leaf manual with regular supplements) ICSA Publishing.

The Charity Commission publishes:

CC1	Charity Commission Publications
CC2	Charities and the Charity Commission
CC3	Responsibilities of Charity Trustees
CC3(a)	Responsibilities of Charity Trustees: A Summary
CC7	Ex Gratia Payments by Charities

The Jelli-babies Protection [League*][Ltd+][Charity]

Jelli-babies House
14 Sweet Lane
Anywhere

Tel: Your ref:
Fax: Our ref:

The Jelli-babies Protection [League*] [Ltd+] [Charity] is registered in England as a company limited by guarantee
Registered No: 123456   Registered Office: as above   *Registered Charity [No:]**

Patron/s: President: #Chairman: Chief Executive:

* Name does not include 'charity' but a statement that it is a registered charity is compliance with s68 of the 1993 Charities Act.
** The inclusion of the charity's registered number is optional.
+ If Ltd does not form part of the company's name a statement usually as a footnote that it is limited or is a limited company is sufficient compliance.
# If any director/trustee of a charitable company is shown on the letterhead, e.g. the name of the chairman, then the names of all the other director/trustees must be stated as well.

30 • HOW TO RUN YOUR CHARITY

COMPANIES HOUSE

Please complete in typescript, or in bold black capitals.

287

Change in situation or address of Registered Office

Company Number

Company Name in full

*F287001**

New situation of registered office

NOTE:

The change in the situation of the registered office does not take effect until the Registrar has registered this notice.

For 14 days beginning with the date that a change of registered office is registered, a person may validly serve any document on the company at its previous registered office.

PO Box numbers only are not acceptable.

Address

Post town

County / Region   Postcode

Signed   Date

† Please delete as appropriate.

† a director / secretary / administrator / administrative receiver / liquidator / receiver manager / receiver

Please give the name, address, telephone number and, if available, a DX number and Exchange of the person Companies House should contact if there is any query.

Tel

DX number   DX exchange

Companies House receipt date barcode

When you have completed and signed the form please send it to the Registrar of Companies at:
Companies House, Crown Way, Cardiff, CF4 3UZ   DX 33050 Cardiff
for companies registered in England and Wales
or
Companies House, 37 Castle Terrace, Edinburgh, EH1 2EB
for companies registered in Scotland   **DX 235 Edinburgh**

Form revised March 1995

SPECIMEN

COMPLIANCE AND THE LAW • 31

288a

COMPANIES HOUSE

Please complete in typescript, or in bold black capitals.

APPOINTMENT of director or secretary
(NOT for resignation (use Form 288b) or change of particulars (use Form 288c))

Company Number

Company Name in full

F288A018

Date of appointment — Day / Month / Year

†Date of Birth — Day / Month / Year

Appointment form
Notes on completion appear on reverse.

Appointment as director / Secretary — *Please mark the appropriate box. If appointment is as a director and secretary mark both boxes.*

NAME
*Style / Title
*Honours etc
Forename(s)
Surname
Previous Forename(s)
Previous Surname
Usual residential address
Post town
Postcode
County / Region
†Nationality
†Business occupation
†Other directorships (additional space overleaf)

I consent to act as ** director / secretary of the above named company

Consent signature   Date

* Voluntary details.
† Directors only.

A director, secretary etc must sign the form below.

Signed   Date

** Please delete as appropriate

(**a director / secretary / administrator / administrative receiver / receiver manager / receiver)

Please give the name, address, telephone number and, if available, a DX number and Exchange of the person Companies House should contact if there is any query.

Tel
DX number   DX exchange

Companies House receipt date barcode

When you have completed and signed the form please send it to the Registrar of Companies at:
Companies House, Crown Way, Cardiff, CF4 3UZ   DX 33050 Cardiff
for companies registered in England and Wales   **or**
Companies House, 37 Castle Terrace, Edinburgh, EH1 2EB
for companies registered in Scotland   DX 235 Edinburgh

Form revised March 1995

SPECIMEN

Company Number ⬚

† Directors only.   †Other directorships ⬚
⬚
⬚
⬚
⬚

SPECIMEN

NOTES
Show the full forenames, NOT INITIALS. If the director or secretary is a corporation or Scottish firm, show the name on surname line and registered or principal office on the usual residential line.

Give previous forenames or surname(s) except:
- for a married woman, the name by which she was known before marriage need not be given.
- for names not used since the age of 18 or for at least 20 years

A peer or individual known by a title may state the title instead of or in addition to the forenames and surname and need not give the name by which that person was known before he or she adopted the title or succeeded to it.

Other directorships.
Give the name of every company incorporated in Great Britain of which the person concerned is a director or has been a director at any time in the past five years.

You may exclude a company which either is, or at all times during the past five years when the person concerned was a director, was
- dormant
- a parent company which wholly owned the company making the return, or
- another wholly owned subsidiary of the same parent company.

COMPLIANCE AND THE LAW • 33

288b

COMPANIES HOUSE

Please complete in typescript, or in bold black capitals.

RESIGNATION of director or secretary
(*NOT for appointment (use Form 288a) or change of particulars (use Form 288c)*)

Company Number

Company Name in full

F288B019

Resignation form

Date of resignation — Day / Month / Year

Resignation as director ☐ as secretary ☐ *Please mark the appropriate box. If resignation is a director and secretary mark both boxes.*

NAME — *Style / Title*

Please insert details as previously notified to Companies House.

Forename(s)

Surname

†Date of Birth — Day / Month / Year

If cessation is other than resignation, please state reason

A serving director, secretary etc must sign the form below.

Signed **Date**

(by a serving director / secretary / administrator / administrative receiver / receiver (manager) receiver)

* Voluntary details.
† Directors only.

Please give the name, address, telephone number and, if available, a DX number and Exchange of the person Companies House should contact if there is any query.

Tel

DX number   DX exchange

Companies House receipt date barcode

When you have completed and signed the form please send it to the Registrar of Companies at:
Companies House, Crown Way, Cardiff, CF4 3UZ   DX 33050 Cardiff
for companies registered in England and Wales   **or**
Companies House, 37 Castle Terrace, Edinburgh, EH1 2EB
for companies registered in Scotland   **DX 235 Edinburgh**

Form revised March 1995

SPECIMEN

34 • HOW TO RUN YOUR CHARITY

COMPANIES HOUSE

288c

Please complete in typescript, or in bold black capitals.

Change of particulars for director or secretary

F288C01A

SPECIMEN

Company Number

Company Name in full

Complete in all cases — Date of change of particulars — Day / Month / Year

Changes of particulars form

Name — *Style / Title

*Honours etc

Forename(s)

Surname

† Date of Birth — Day / Month / Year

Change of name (enter new name) — Forename(s)

Surname

Change of usual residential address (enter new address)

Post town

County / Region

Postcode

Country

Other change (please specify)

A serving director, secretary etc must sign the form below.

Signed

Date

(by a serving director / secretary / administrator / administrative receiver / receiver manager / receiver)

* Voluntary details.
† Directors only.

Please give the name, address, telephone number and, if available, a DX number and Exchange of the person Companies House should contact if there is any query.

Tel

DX number

DX exchange

When you have completed and signed the form please send it to the Registrar of Companies at:
Companies House, Crown Way, Cardiff, CF4 3UZ   DX 33050 Cardiff
for companies registered in England and Wales   **or**
Companies House, 37 Castle Terrace, Edinburgh, EH1 2EB
for companies registered in Scotland   **DX 235 Edinburgh**

Form revised March 1995

3

MANAGEMENT AND ORGANISATION

3.1 Trustees

Status

Those individuals who have the responsibility for ensuring that a charity carries out its purpose and objectives lawfully and in accordance with its governing document are its trustees. Every charity is a trust in the literal sense of that word. However not every charity trustee will be aware that he is a trustee with legal responsibilities. This confusion is partly due to the fact that trustees are often described in a variety of different ways. They may for example be described as members of the executive committee, management committee, council or the board. If the charity is incorporated as a company limited by guarantee then it is the directors who are the trustees and consequently have a dual role as both director and trustee: hence the term director/trustee.

Usually the rules which apply to a charity formed as an unincorporated association will be set out in a trust deed or written constitution. In the case of a charitable company its constitution is its memorandum and articles of association. There are also a few charities whose constitution stems from a Royal Charter. Some charities are governed by a specific Act of Parliament but these are very few. The term used in this book for a charity's constitution however constituted is the governing document.

Custodian or holding trustees

There is often misunderstanding over the term custodian or holding trustee. The role of a custodian or holding trustee is simply to hold the legal title to an unincorporated charity's property or investments. In that sense the role is purely functional and a holding trustee does not have any responsibility (or liability for that matter) for carrying out the charity's purpose and objectives.

Holding trustees are subject to the instructions of the trustees of the charity, provided of course that such instructions are not unlawful. In the case of a charitable company there would not be any need to appoint custodian or holding trustees as any property would normally be held in the name of the company itself.

Choice of charity trustees and the ideal personal qualities they should possess

The secretary will usually be involved in any discussions leading to the appointment of an additional or replacement trustee. Not everyone wishes to be a charity trustee or has the appropriate qualities and experience.

Charity trustees should primarily be appointed for what they can contribute in experience and knowledge and ideally some trustees should have business skills and experience. It is not necessarily sensible for a trustee to be appointed simply because of his status or position in a particular locality or community. Such figurehead trustees should instead be appointed as patrons or similar.

To ensure that a trustee fulfils the role properly he should be able to devote sufficient time and commitment to the charity. Trustees who have experience which is particularly relevant to the aims and objectives of their charity make ideal appointments, although it is important to ensure that in any group of trustees there is a blend of complementary skills and attributes as well as a mix of personalities which can be quite difficult to achieve. Trustees also have general responsibility for upholding the principles of good governance – more of which in Chapter 5.

Qualification for appointment

Anyone aged 18 or over who is not bankrupt and who is not a patient as defined by the mental health legislation can act as a trustee of a charity. Sometimes a charity's governing document will prescribe particular qualifications or other qualities a trustee should possess, which may for example be a specific religious belief or residential qualification, or a maximum age. Some charity trustees are appointed directly as a result of their involvement with another organisation, for example a local authority or other public body.

Appointment

The first trustees are usually those who have either promoted or sponsored the charity to the point of its inception. The governing document may state specifically by name who the initial trustees will be or how they are to be appointed.

A trustee is more likely to discharge his responsibilities effectively if prior to or on appointment he acquires some knowledge of the objectives and purposes of the charity as well as an understanding of the procedures which govern the way in which a trustee can act. A newly appointed trustee should for example be able to assess the resources which are available to the charity and if it owns property, the condition of that property. For a structured induction programme appropriate for a newly appointed trustee see section 1.3.

Retirement and re-appointment

Although trustees are usually appointed for a specific term, maybe for only a year, they are normally eligible for re-appointment. Sometimes the governing document will state that a trustee can only be re-appointed for a finite period of time following which he must then retire – see clause 24 of Appendix 1 and clause 44 of Appendix 2. Retirement and re-appointment as a trustee will usually be in accordance with:

- ☐ the provisions contained in the governing document; or
- ☐ the Trustee Act 1925 unless it is excluded by the governing document; or
- ☐ by the Charity Commission; or
- ☐ exceptionally by the court.

Removal of trustees

The removal of charity trustees is regulated by:

- ☐ the provisions contained in the governing document; or
- ☐ the Trustee Act 1925; or
- ☐ the Charities Act 1993; or
- ☐ the Charity Commission; or
- ☐ the court, but this is very unusual.

Strictly speaking a check should be made to ensure that a prospective trustee of a charity is not liable to be disqualified by virtue of the Charities Act 1993. Sections 72–3 of the 1993 Act disqualify any of the following unless the Commission decides to waive such disqualification:

- ☐ A person convicted of a criminal offence of dishonesty unless the conviction is spent as defined by the Rehabilitation of Offenders Act 1974.
- ☐ An undischarged bankrupt.
- ☐ A person disqualified from being a company director.

General approach by trustees to their role

There are no hard and fast rules as to what the approach should be. It is probably sensible for trustees new and existing to make enquiries about the kind of work which is being done by charities and voluntary organisations operating in the same or similar area of activity. Charities with common aims may combine to form a loose association or umbrella organisation to help co-ordinate their work. So far as practicable, trustees should co-operate with other charities and exchange information in order to maximise the use of resources and avoid duplication. The overriding consideration however is that trustees must ensure that what they do and the decisions they make are in accordance with the aims and objectives of their own charity's governing document.

3.2 Powers of trustees

Principles

The guiding principle is that trustees must exercise their powers strictly in accordance with their charity's own governing document. However, certain powers are also derived from statute, in particular the Charities Act 1993 and the law of trusts and equity as developed by the courts over many years.

Delegation

Trustees should act in person and any policy decisions concerning their charity must be taken by the trustees acting together as a body. There is no implied power to delegate although trustees can nominate some of their number to consider particular matters or specific items of business and to make recommendations, but the decision as to whether or not to act as recommended is for the trustees to take together. The minutes of any meetings of a sub-committee or reports should be circulated to all trustees as a matter of course.

It is not appropriate for an individual trustee to be allocated a specific part of the income of a charity or to manage a particular aspect of the charity's activity alone. A charity's governing document may however authorise the setting up of committees or sub-committees to deal with certain elements of the charity's activities and generally this is sensible and pragmatic provided the governing body of trustees is kept adequately and regularly informed. It is usually good practice for a member of the governing body to chair any sub-committee and any working group in order to provide a direct link with the trustees as a whole.

Generally trustees are responsible for the overall management and strategy of their charity even though the day-to-day responsibility may (but not always) be delegated wholly or in part to either honorary officers or employed staff, or a combination of the two. The scope of any delegated authority should be clearly laid down in writing and particular items of business must be referred back to the trustees acting collectively as the governing body to make the final decision. The trustees remain legally responsible and must therefore supervise and control the work of employees and volunteers.

Investment

In the absence of anything to the contrary in a charity's governing document the power of its trustees to invest is governed by the Trustee Investments Act 1961 as amended by the Charities (Trustee Investments Act) Order 1995. The 1961 Act is, however, restrictive and if a charity wishes to invest its funds more widely the charity's governing document should contain the necessary power extending the range of investments the trustees can make. The law generally on this topic is in the process of further review and is likely to be reformed although progress was delayed by the 1997 General Election.

Other powers

A number of other powers are available to trustees by virtue of the Charities Act 1993. Examples include the power for the trustees of a small charity to transfer all its property to another charity or for very small charities to spend their capital subject to certain rules – see Charity Commission leaflet CC44. A small charity is one with an annual income of less than £5,000 not being an exempt charity nor a charitable company. Nonetheless trustees are advised to take legal advice and if appropriate consult the Commission if they are contemplating any action which is not clearly and specifically within the powers contained in the charity's own governing document or permitted by the 1993 Act.

3.3 Duties of trustees

Protection of property and other assets

Trustees have a duty to protect their charity's property. They must ensure the charity continues to be effective as well as solvent and in particular preserve any endowed funds or property.

If a charity owns leasehold or freehold property its trustees should check on a continuing basis the condition of that property and whether or not anything is happening to it which could cause difficulty in the future; for example the deterioration in the fabric of a building or failing to take action over a letting which has proved to be unsuitable.

There is also a continuing duty to ensure that all of a charity's assets are insured and that any other necessary or appropriate insurance cover is effected and maintained. Matters relating to insurance are dealt with in Chapter 8.

Financial and administrative control

Charity trustees must exercise general control over their charity's financial affairs and they should ensure that the way in which the charity is administered is not open to abuse by dishonest employees or others associated with the charity. They have the further duty to check that any administrative or other systems of financial control are rigorous and constantly maintained and where possible improved. Although the day-to-day responsibility for administration can be delegated to the secretary, honorary or otherwise, depending on the size of the organisation, ultimate responsibility rests with the trustees. This is dealt with in more detail in Chapter 11.

Money which is not needed for immediate expenditure must be invested in order to earn interest. Any investments should be reviewed periodically to make sure that not only do such investments continue to be suitable so far as the charity is concerned but also the type of investment meets the charity's needs. It is preferable that bank accounts should be operated by at least two trustees (or perhaps one trustee and the secretary) and not left to a single trustee or other authorised individual.

No conflict of interest

A trustee must not place himself in a position where his personal interest could conflict with that of the charity. A trustee should not therefore profit in any way from his trusteeship unless in exceptional circumstances special permission has been sought and given – see section 3.7 below. Nonetheless a trustee is entitled to be reimbursed any reasonable expenses properly incurred due to his work as a trustee. It should however be noted that the articles of association of many charitable companies allow a director/trustee to be interested in a contract with the charitable company provided that he declares such interest. This is perhaps contradictory given the general prohibition against a trustee receiving any benefit from his position as a trustee. Consequently any such provision should be very carefully monitored and not abused if exercised.

Any trustee should also as a matter of course familiarise himself fully with the details and workings of the charity's governing document.

Accounting records

As already mentioned, trustees also have a duty to make sure that proper books of account and other financial records are kept and retained for the six-year period.

Registration

Trustees of a qualifying charity in England and Wales must ensure that it is registered in accordance with the Charities Act 1993, and as already mentioned that an annual return is made to the Commission as prescribed by the 1993 Act and also to the Registrar if the charity is constituted as a charitable company.

Compliance with aims and objectives

There is of course the overriding duty on the part of trustees to ensure that the charity's activities accord with its aims and objectives and are carried out within the terms of its governing document. If this should prove impossible to achieve or perhaps more expensive than it need be then the trustees are bound to request the Commission for directions as to how any difficulty can or should be overcome and if appropriate to apply for a scheme to be devised by the Commission. The Charity Commission's leaflet on this topic is CC36.

3.4 Liability of trustees

Breach of trust

Trustees are personally liable for the consequences if they act in a way which constitutes a breach of trust. Where for example trustees allow monies to be used for purposes not permitted by the governing document or where they fail to act reasonably and the charity suffers financial loss as a result, they may be personally liable for breach of trust *regardless* of whether the charity is incorporated or unincorporated. Hence charity trustees who for example sanction unlawful political campaigning activities are potentially at risk to make good the money improperly spent.

A salutary example involved the former trustees of War on Want. In this case the trustees were required by the Commission to repay the charity £37,000 over ten years because the Commission considered that an advertisement placed by the trustees had been too political in content. In its report which was issued in 1991, the Commission also dealt with various examples of mismanagement and of a general breakdown in organisation.

If charity trustees are uncertain whether a proposed course of action is permitted, they should seek specialist legal advice or consult the

Commission direct. If the trustees provide the Commission with a full account of the facts and obtain written advice from them under s. 29 of the 1993 Act, the trustees will be protected from any possible future charge or accusation of breach of trust. Moreover, if it can be shown that a trustee has acted reasonably and in all the circumstances ought fairly to be excused, the courts or the Commission also have the power to exonerate him from personal liability for breach of trust.

Contract

If a charity is *unincorporated*, the absence of limited liability exposes the trustees to the additional potential risk of being liable for damages as a result of a breach of contract.

Third parties

In the case of an unincorporated charity (virtually any charity which is not a charitable company), the trustees are collectively and individually personally (which in practice means financially) liable for all negligent acts and omissions causing injury or loss where a duty of care is owed to third parties.

Indemnity

Where trustees have acted in accordance with their charity's governing document, they will normally have the right to be indemnified out of the assets of the charity. Such assets may, however, be insufficient and so trustees are advised to try and limit their liability by, for example, the careful drafting of contracts, and here legal advice is important.

Leases

There have been a number of cases where trustees have been sued by landlords in respect of leases taken out in the individual names of the trustees. So far as leases entered into after 1 January 1996 are concerned, this should not be so much of a problem as the Landlord and Tenant (Covenants) Act 1995 came into force on that date. The Act largely does away with the rule of privity of contract in leases. The effect of this rule meant that where a landlord granted a lease of his property he was able to enforce the obligations under the lease against those named in it even if the lease had been assigned in the meantime to a third party. If an assignee did not pay the rent the landlord would not only be able to enforce the terms of the lease against the defaulting assignee but against the original tenant because of privity of contract.

For new leases granted after 1 January 1996 a tenant may be released from his obligations to the landlord when he assigns the lease. The same will apply to any person who stood as surety or guarantor for the tenant. There are, however, still some provisions which will protect landlords in the future. The landlord can under the new Act require an assigning tenant to enter into an authorised guarantee agreement to guarantee the performance by the assignee of his obligations under the lease if a stipulation to that effect is contained in the lease itself. However as mentioned above in the case of any lease entered into before 1 January 1996, the risk of potential liability to a charity trustee who is named in the lease remains if an assignee of the lease subsequently defaults.

Wrongful trading

Limited liability offers some protection to trustees, at least as regards liability to third parties. However, the benefit of limited liability is not absolute. For example, a director/trustee of a charitable company is subject to the consequences if he is a party to fraudulent or wrongful trading in contravention of the Insolvency Act 1986. This comes as something of a surprise to many director/trustees unfamiliar with the legislation.

Insurance

One possible (but not necessarily foolproof) way to protect trustees is for the charity to effect trustee liability insurance. The Commission may agree that in some cases the premiums can be paid out of a charity's funds. The Commission has published leaflet CC49 on this topic. A charitable company can in principle acquire such insurance cover for its director/trustees because it is permitted to do so by companies legislation. However, the company's memorandum and articles of association will need to be amended if the necessary power is not already included. Similarly, in the case of an unincorporated charity the consent of the Commission will be required to include an appropriate provision in its governing document if not already included. It will also be necessary to show in every case that the insurance is in the interests of the charity generally and not only in the interests of the trustees.

3.5 Transfer of title to property on retirement of a trustee

Where the trustees of an unincorporated charity who are to retire hold property, whether freehold or leasehold, in their own names, it is important to ensure that such property is transferred by any retiring trustee(s) into the names of the continuing (if any) and any incoming trustee(s). The reason for this is that the retirement or removal of a trustee does not of itself transfer the title to property out of the names of the retiring trustee(s) and into the name(s) of any incoming trustee(s). Legal assistance will almost certainly be required to deal with a transfer.

3.6 Honorary officers

Definition of 'honorary'

The term 'honorary' means that anyone who is appointed on such a basis carries out his duties without payment apart from entitlement to reimbursement of expenses. The description is frequently misused in practice.

Various charity appointments are of an honorary nature, for example president, vice-president, chairman and vice-chairman. Other individuals may perform an honorary role, for example a surveyor if the charity owns land or buildings. In most charities the secretary and the treasurer act in an honorary capacity although either of these two appointments may be held by paid employees if the charity is large enough.

President

This is perhaps a somewhat grandiose title for a charity. The rationale is that it is likely to be beneficial to a charity for someone of prominence to fulfil this role, which varies in significance from one charity to another. The responsibility may be limited to chairing the annual general meeting and perhaps any other general meetings. Ideally the appointment of such an individual should assist the charity in attracting funds and perhaps positive publicity. Although there are contrary points of view as to the status of a president of a charity, he is likely to be regarded as a trustee. In the case of a charitable company notification of the appointment should be sent to Companies House on form 288a.

Vice-President

A charity which is established to assist for example former services personnel and their dependants, may appoint as vice-presidents a number of distinguished high ranking individuals who have retired from the services. They would perhaps be drawn from the three armed forces and therefore represent the interests of each. In most cases they would be regarded as trustees. The appointment of a vice-president of a charitable company should also be notified to Companies House on form 288a.

Chairman

The chairmanship of the governing body is clearly a very important position, and the appointee should be able to demonstrate powers of leadership and strategic thinking. Again the role of the chairman will vary from one charity to another depending on its size and complexity and the extent of the chairman's day-to-day involvement. Difficulties can arise, however, where there is a part-time chairman and a full-time chief executive or similar, because their respective roles would have to be very clearly defined to ensure as far as possible that there was minimal scope for conflict.

Vice-Chairman

This role is also important because someone should be nominated to deputise for the chairman if he is unavailable. The role of vice-chairman may also include chairing the charity's committees if there are any.

Secretary

The secretary, apart from fulfilling the core duties and responsibilities already referred to, may take on a broader function depending on the size and nature of the charity. In some charities the secretary may also act as the controller, general manager or chief executive. The secretary may be on a par with other senior employees, for example the financial controller or the director of operations. It is very unlikely that a full-time secretary would act in an honorary capacity.

Treasurer

In the smaller charity the honorary treasurer will supervise the keeping of the financial accounts and will operate the bank accounts as well as looking after the assets of the charity. He will probably be involved in recommending how any surplus funds are invested. He will also prepare periodic financial statements and budgets for consideration by the trustees.

In contrast, the full-time treasurer or financial controller of a large charity will also be a paid official, and his role and responsibilities will be similar to those of the treasurer or chief accountant/financial controller of a large commercial undertaking. In such larger charities the paid official may be described as the finance director. Nonetheless the honorary treasurer of the larger charity will still have the very important role to fulfil of monitoring the finances of the charity in conjunction with the finance director and accounting staff and will report to the governing body on financial matters.

3.7 Remuneration of charity trustees

Basic principles

There are two basic principles which have to be taken into account when deciding if charity trustees are entitled to receive payment other than the reimbursement of their out-of-pocket expenses.

The first is that charities exist for the public benefit and therefore charity trustees must not act in a way which would either give them a personal advantage or result in financial gain. The second principle is that a charity must be properly administered in accordance with its objectives. It is therefore necessary that anyone who wishes to be a charity trustee should not only have the appropriate experience but be able to give sufficient time to the role.

Legal principles

The question of whether or not charity trustees should be remunerated is a vexed one and has been reviewed by the courts from time to time. There is also the question of whether or not paid employees can or should be appointed as trustees of their employing charity. Another factor to be considered is the type and size of the organisation because the diversity is enormous.

On the one hand a charity may be a single trust which holds capital and collects and dispenses income periodically, and on the other it may be a substantial undertaking providing an extensive range of services and comprising many individuals, employees as well as volunteers. Charities which fall into the latter category are usually large and complex operations which have to be structured and managed in a business-like way.

If trustees do not have the necessary expertise they can obtain and pay for appropriate professional advice or services. Trustees can also employ staff and appoint agents. However the basic principle is that a trustee takes on the role gratuitously and as such does not have an automatic right or entitlement to payment. Although the courts have declared that payment in certain circumstances may be made it can only be done (in most cases) where it is shown that it is not only necessary and reasonable but it is also in the best interests of the charity. It would therefore be up to the trustees to show that payment is both necessary and reasonable.

The Commission can refuse to register a new charity if the objects for which it is to be established are not exclusively charitable. Although the governing document of a charity applying for registration can include provision for the remuneration of its trustees, if the level of payment is out of proportion to the contribution to be made, the trustees could be considered to be beneficiaries. If that were to be the case the organisation may not be accepted by the Commission as being exclusively charitable. If, however, payment is limited to an amount which is reasonable in relation to the services which are to be provided by a trustee the charity should, other things being equal, be registered.

Existing charities

If the charity's governing document (and particularly in the case of a charitable company its memorandum and articles of association) allows remuneration to be paid to its trustees or director/trustees as the case may be, such power can be exercised but strictly in conformity with the terms laid down in the governing document.

If the governing document does not contain an express power the general rule is that the trustees are not entitled to receive anything at all for their services to the charity. Even if there is a provision in the governing document which allows it to be amended this procedure could not be invoked to enable the trustees to be remunerated in the future. To attempt such an amendment could potentially put the trustees in breach of their fiduciary duty as the consequences of such a change would be to grant the trustees a personal benefit. Any proposal to make a change would in any event require the consent of the Commission.

In the case of a charitable company s. 64 of the Charities Act 1993 provides that in specific cases a company is not able to alter its memorandum and articles of association or even pass the necessary special resolution without the *prior written approval* of the Commission. See also page 82.

Power of the Charity Commission to authorise payment to trustees

The Commission can authorise the payment of remuneration to charity trustees in specific and individual cases. The Commission, in exercising its discretion, will apply the guidelines and principles which the courts have developed as well as taking into account the particular circumstances of the case. Some of the factors which the Commission would bear in mind are the size of the charity, its structure, the way in which it operates and the extent to which the trustees undertake administrative obligations. Consequently, when an application is made to the Commission requesting consent to pay a charity trustee such application should be fairly detailed.

Factors relevant to a request for remuneration

The following are examples of what the Commission would be looking for when it considers an application by trustees:

- ☐ Any power to pay remuneration contained in the governing document.
- ☐ The size and structure of the charity.
- ☐ The nature of the charity's activities.
- ☐ The degree of involvement by the trustees.
- ☐ The specialist nature of the skills required.
- ☐ The comparative costs of obtaining specialist skills.

Payment for services provided by professionally qualified trustees

If an individual trustee is a member of a profession, for example an accountant or a solicitor, and the trustees wish to remunerate him or his firm not in his role as a trustee but for work carried out for the charity in a *professional* capacity, the trustees can do so provided there is an express provision to that effect in the charity's governing document. If the governing document does not contain such a provision then the trustees in their application to the Commission will have to justify any proposed payment by reference to the criteria set out on page 46 above.

Paying an honorarium to a trustee

It quite often happens that a trustee of a smaller charity will take on an additional role such as secretary or treasurer and consequently be paid an honorarium for such work. The honorarium is usually pitched at a token amount and is less than would be charged by someone carrying out such work professionally. Nonetheless any payment to a trustee for whatever reason has to be authorised either by the charity's governing document or by the Commission.

Remuneration for particular work

Trustees can ask the Commission for consent specifically to pay one or more of their number to undertake particular work for the charity. In such a case the trustees would have to be able to show that:

- ☐ The work was exceptional.
- ☐ The work was necessary.
- ☐ The payment was bona fide, which means that the amount was not any more than it would have been if someone else had been employed to carry out the work.
- ☐ The amount was commensurate with the work to be performed.

If all of these conditions are satisfied then the Commission will probably authorise the payment by an order under s. 26 of the 1993 Act.

Employment of staff

In some cases the trustees are unable to deal with the administration and management of the charity themselves and the only practical arrangement is for the charity itself to employ staff. If staff are employed it does not necessarily follow that a trustee cannot claim payment for work done by him instead of an employee. It would still be the responsibility of the trustees to supervise employees because a charity cannot be run properly if all responsibility is delegated to employees and the trustees cease to be involved at all.

Trustees who are paid directors of an associated trading company

Quite a few charities have associated non-charitable trading companies which are wholly owned subsidiaries of the charity. A charity trustee who is also a director of such a trading company can retain the fees payable to him as a director but only if the charity's own governing document expressly allows this to be done. If not, then a trustee would have to obtain the consent of the Commission to retain any fees received by him as a director of the trading company. Otherwise the retention of fees would amount to a receipt by the trustee of a benefit to which he was not entitled. Consequently the director would have to account to the 'parent' charity for any fees received.

Claiming expenses

All that has been mentioned so far does *not* apply to the reimbursement of out-of-pocket expenses which have been properly and reasonably incurred by a trustee in carrying out his responsibilities as a trustee of the charity.

3.8 Director/trustees of a charitable company

Definition of a 'director' and 'shadow director'

The Companies Act 1985 defines 'director' as including any person occupying the position of director by whatever name called. In relation to a limited company, 'shadow director' means a person in accordance with whose directions or instructions the directors of the company are accustomed to act. See also pages 51–2 below.

It should be noted, however, that a person would not normally be regarded as a director if he gives advice as a professional consultant. A director/trustee, it should be emphasised, is an officer of the company and therefore liable to incur various penalties personally if he or the company is in default with regard to the numerous obligations imposed by the Companies Acts 1985–89 and the Insolvency Act 1986. A director/trustee is not entitled to any latitude under the Companies Acts merely because he happens to be a director/trustee of a charitable company.

Qualification and appointment of a director/trustee

The qualification and appointment of a director/trustee is partly governed by the provisions of the 1985 Act and partly by what is contained in the company's articles of association. In practice it would be quite usual for the existing director/trustees to appoint an additional director/trustee during the course of a year, provided the specified number (if any) who can be appointed as director/trustees is not exceeded. A newly appointed director/trustee would hold office until the next annual general meeting at which he would have to retire although normally he would be eligible for re-election.

The articles of association of some charitable companies provide that all director/trustees retire each year, and not just one-third, but that they are all eligible for re-election. There may, however, be a time bar which would normally be five years – see clauses 43/4 of Appendix 2. It is a common misconception that all directors of limited companies have to retire by rotation; this is so only if the articles of association include such a requirement.

The minutes of the meeting at which a director/trustee is appointed should record such appointment. The secretary must then complete form 288a with the details of the new appointee. Once this has been done the procedure is as follows:

☐ The director/trustee signs form 288a consenting to his appointment.
☐ The secretary or a director/trustee countersigns the form and inserts the appropriate date.
☐ The secretary sends the form to Companies House.
☐ The secretary then enters the details of the newly appointed director/trustee in the register of director/trustees.

A letter in similar terms to the model draft on page 63 should be sent to a newly appointed director/trustee.

There is no obligation to notify the Commission of the appointment of a new director/trustee but the opportunity will arise for this information to be included in the annual return. It should also be decided whether the newly appointed director/trustee is to be a signatory to the charity's bank account, in which case this should be minuted and arrangements made with the bank to amend the mandate.

The director/trustee's general duty of care

Director/trustees are agents of their charitable company. In that capacity they have the duty of carrying out the whole of the purpose for which the company has been established, subject to any restrictions imposed by the articles of association and any statutory provisions. In exercising their powers director/trustees owe a duty to their company to make decisions without fear or favour.

The director/trustee of a charitable company is bound by the general duties of trustees referred to in section 3.3 above. However, he is also subject to the duties which have been established by case law in the courts dealing with the legal position and responsibilities of directors generally. In one case concerning a commercial company it was declared that a director is expected to show the degree of skill which can reasonably be expected from a person of his knowledge and experience, or in other words the level of competence relevant to him as an individual. This is on the face of it paradoxical, as it would appear that a lesser standard of competence is required of a director of a commercial company than is required of a director/trustee of a charitable company. A director/trustee should therefore expect to achieve the higher level of competence required of a charity trustee generally, which is another example of an anomaly existing between company law and trust law.

Director/trustees must also comply with an additional set of duties known as fiduciary duties which have been developed by the courts over many years. The fiduciary duties of a director/trustee are:

☐ To exercise his powers bona fide for the purposes for which they were conferred, i.e. for the benefit of the company as a whole.
☐ In the event of a situation arising where he is or will be directly or indirectly interested in any contract or other dealing with the company, to notify the company of that fact as soon as practicable.
☐ To refrain from putting himself in a position in which his duties and his personal interests may conflict.
☐ In the event of making a personal gain to reimburse the company.

It will be appreciated that there are broad similarities between these fiduciary duties and the duty of care required of trustees as a general rule, although in the case of director/trustees the position has been spelt out to some extent more specifically. For example, if a director/trustee is interested in a contract with a charitable company he must disclose his interest as required by s. 317 of the 1985 Act and will generally be precluded from voting in respect of the contract – see clause 42 of Appendix 2 and note also that failure to declare such interest may constitute a ground for disqualification and removal of the director/trustee.

Shadow director/trustees

Can the director/trustee of a charitable company ever be regarded as a shadow director/trustee? In principle perhaps he can, because of the definition of 'director' given in the 1985 Act already mentioned in on page 49 above – a definition which includes any person occupying the position of director however described. Some sections of the 1985 Act extend the scope of the meaning to include any person in accordance with whose instructions the directors of the company are accustomed to act. The term used to describe such individuals is 'shadow director', and this is another area of potential conflict between company law and trust law. There is no concept of a 'shadow trustee' of an unincorporated charity or, for that matter, a charity established by Royal Charter.

A professional adviser to a charitable company will not usually be treated as a shadow director provided he does no more than advise, leaving the director/trustees to make the final decision on the matters to be resolved.

Liability of director/trustees

The same principles apply to a director/trustee as they do to the secretary with regard to liability for breaches of various aspects of company legislation. The imposition of a fine may, for example, occur as a result of the failure by a director/trustee to file a charitable company's annual accounts with the Registrar at the proper time. Where court proceedings have been instituted, the court, as already mentioned, has power to waive penalties in certain circumstances. In many cases a breach of the law can lead to the imposition of a term of imprisonment or a fine or both.

The Insolvency Act 1986 in principle applies to charitable companies even though it was primarily designed to deal with insolvent commercial trading companies. In the event of a charitable company continuing to operate while it is insolvent, with no reasonable prospect of its financial position being retrieved, with the result that wrongful trading occurs, a director/trustee could be ordered by the court to contribute personally towards the losses incurred by the company if the liquidator applies for the appropriate order. There are no reported cases at present of this happening but there could come a time when it does, particularly where a charitable company takes on a quasi-business role as a consequence of the 'contract culture'.

Persons disqualified from being director/trustees

The Company Directors Disqualification Act 1986 provides that a person may be disqualified from being a director of a limited company (including a charitable company) for the following reasons:

- ☐ If he is an undischarged bankrupt, unless the court gave its permission for him to continue as a director at the time he was made bankrupt.

- By the court if the person:
  - has been convicted of an offence in connection with the promotion, formation, management or liquidation of a company or with the receivership or management of a company's property; or
  - in the course of a winding up of a company is found to be guilty of fraudulent trading or breach of duty towards the company whilst an officer, liquidator, receiver or manager; or
  - has persistently been in default in making returns or delivering accounts or any other document required by companies legislation. If there have been three convictions for such failure within a five-year period this would be regarded as conclusive evidence of persistent default.

The court must also make a disqualification order if it is satisfied that a person is or has been a director of a company which has at any time become insolvent and his conduct as a director of that company makes him unfit to be concerned with the management of a company.

Retirement of director/trustees

The articles of association quite often state (but not necessarily as already mentioned) that one-third of the director/trustees are to retire at each annual general meeting and that those to retire in each year are those who have been longest in office since their last election. A retiring director/trustee is usually eligible for re-election although that may not always be the case.

The articles usually include a provision setting out the circumstances in which a director/trustee would be disqualified from continuing to act. He may for example be disqualified if he resigns his office by notice in writing or in circumstances where he is directly or indirectly interested in a contract with the company but failed to declare the nature of that interest as required by the 1985 Act. Sometimes the articles will also provide that if a director/trustee fails to attend a certain number of meetings he can be disqualified.

The articles may also provide that a director/trustee must retire on reaching a certain age but if there is no such provision he can continue in office so long as he is re-elected periodically, assuming that the articles provide for director/trustees retiring by rotation to be re-elected. Sometimes the articles state that a director/trustee can only be re-elected for a certain period of time following the conclusion of which he must retire – see clause 44 of Appendix 2. There are however various conflicting views as to whether or not such a provision is either sensible or appropriate.

As noted on page 50 above, a director/trustee who is appointed during the year must retire at the next annual general meeting following his appointment so that he can be formally elected by the members.

Removal of a director/trustee

A director/trustee of a charitable company may be removed from office before he would normally retire if the members in general meeting pass an ordinary resolution to that effect. An ordinary resolution is one which is approved by a simple majority of those members who attend and vote at a meeting which has been properly convened for the purpose.

Compensation for loss of office as a director/trustee

Charity trustees are not entitled to receive compensation for loss of office, and the same generally applies to a director/trustee of a charitable company who is removed from office.

However, the 1993 Act does specifically provide that the prior written consent of the Commission must be obtained if a charitable company intends to make a payment to a director/trustee in respect of loss of office or retirement, or a payment in respect of loss of office or retirement made in connection with the transfer of the company's undertaking or property, or it is proposed to incorporate into a director/trustee's service contract a term whereby his employment may continue for a period of more than five years. As already mentioned, no trustee except in particular circumstances can profit personally from his position as a trustee.

The 1993 Act strengthens the control of the Commission over charitable companies to prevent director/trustees from carrying out certain transactions which would otherwise be permissible under companies legislation.

The criminal law and director/trustees

Director/trustees of charitable companies can be prosecuted if they commit various criminal acts. They may for example be liable for theft of property from the company or for false accounting. They may also be liable if they make false statements. In addition, if a charitable company obtains property or a pecuniary advantage by deception and the offence is proved to have been committed with the consent or connivance of a director/trustee he will be guilty of the offence as well as the charitable company.

As will already have been noted, the Companies Acts 1985–89, the Insolvency Act 1986 and the Company Directors Disqualification Act 1986 all include many provisions, breach of which would make a director/trustee liable to criminal sanction by way of a fine or imprisonment or both. In addition, if a charitable company carries on its activity with the intention of defrauding its creditors, every person knowingly a party to such an intention would be liable on conviction to imprisonment of up to seven years or a fine or both. Director/trustees may also be liable to be convicted for breaches of the health and safety at work legislation and regulations.

3.9 Honorary advisers

From time to time charity trustees will require advice and professional services depending on the nature of the charity's objects and purpose. For example, a charity which provides residential accommodation for elderly or infirm residents may have as a member of its governing body someone with a medical or nursing background. Such individuals should preferably be prepared to give their advice on a general basis and attend most if not all meetings of the trustees.

A charity should preferably have an established procedure for appointing and re-appointing honorary advisers. It is important that they remain active in their particular field of expertise otherwise their knowledge can soon become out of date. It may be generally sensible for all honorary advisers to retire after a specific period – say three years – and if still required then asked to continue if willing to do so.

3.10 Employees

Employee responsibility

As charities have grown in size and complexity so has the need increased to employ staff. It will not be forgotten that it is a fundamental principle of trusteeship that trustees cannot benefit personally from their role as charity trustees. Consequently, as a general rule no employee or other person who receives remuneration can be a member of a charity's governing body other than in the special cases approved by the Commission as mentioned in section 3.7.

Staff can be employed to implement the policy decided by the trustees and unless the charity's governing document stipulates to the contrary an employee may be a member of a committee which has been given responsibility for day-to-day management. The expertise of employees may also be important in helping to develop the charity's policy and objectives which are ultimately agreed or endorsed by the governing body. Staff are usually employed to deal with the considerable volume of administrative and secretarial work which can be generated particularly by the larger charity. Employees also provide a range of professional skills – managerial, financial, educational, or medical – so that the charity is able to achieve its objectives and carry out its purpose more effectively.

Senior employees of a large charity

The staff will usually be led by a chief executive or similar individual. Such a person may also be the secretary, or secretary and controller, or secretary general, or director, or perhaps be described in some other way depending on the charity's size and the nature of its organisation. If the title of director is used by the chief executive of a charitable company it would be advisable to make it clear particularly on the charity's notepaper and other stationery that it is only the members of the governing body who are the director/trustees.

The chief executive of a charity should possess a number of qualities, the more important ones being:

- ☐ Flair and imagination in utilising effectively all the resources of the charity including staff, volunteers, money and other property.
- ☐ Sensitivity to the needs of those beneficiaries entitled to seek assistance.
- ☐ A talent for establishing in conjunction with the trustees and other staff a positive cost-effective and creative response to the needs and requirements of beneficiaries.
- ☐ The ability to communicate effectively both orally and in writing.

Charities nowadays must have effective management particularly in the areas of finance, marketing, fund-raising and publicity. To achieve this, experienced and competent employees will be required, but as with much else, the need will depend upon the size, scope and ambitions of the particular charity. Senior staff should be able to demonstrate not only a wide range of skills but also the ability to deal competently with the governing body, its committees (if any), volunteers, beneficiaries, donors, local/central government and, not least, other colleagues and employees. The ability to cope with the press, radio and television media may also be necessary.

3.11 The relationship between trustees, employees and volunteers

General considerations

Good working relationships between trustees, employees and volunteers are self-evidently very important to the effective management of a charity. It is an aspect which can often be overlooked or ignored when relationships change as the charity expands into a corporate entity employing many individuals grouped into various departments, each with its own manager. Superimposed on this is the potential for strains to develop between experienced employees and the governing body of voluntary trustees.

On the one hand the trustees will acknowledge their need to rely on experienced employees in running a large organisation but on the other they will be very conscious of their authority which derives from their position as trustees and their accountability, not only to the Charity Commission (and in the case of a charitable company the Registrar of Companies) but also to the wider world.

The responsibility for setting policy and seeing that it is implemented lies with the trustees, and in a very small charity they may also be personally responsible for implementation. In the case of a medium-sized charity the trustees may be able, at least to some extent, to delegate the implementation of policy to others. There is likely to be a close working relationship between the trustees of such a charity and others who are involved with it, and consequently policy may develop collectively as well as being implemented jointly. In the larger charity a more formal process will need to be established by which policy is decided and its implementation monitored. Whatever approach is adopted certain principles govern the formation of effective working relationships.

It is important that larger charities should study carefully these basic principles so that voluntary groups and employees at all levels can best work together in achieving the charity's objectives and at the same time remember that it is the trustees who have the ultimate legal responsibility for the conduct of the charity's affairs. If things go wrong it is the trustees who are accountable – the 'buck' stops with them.

Trustees and employees

The terms of reference and the job description of the chief executive should give as much scope as is reasonably practicable for the development of the work of the charity within the policy laid down by the trustees. The trustees can best retain control of the way in which their policy is being carried out by requiring periodic reports from the chief executive as to progress. In addition, the trustees can set limits on financial expenditure and particularly in a large organisation the trustees may wish to be involved in the recruitment of senior staff. It is important that lines of authority are clearly defined and reviewed from time to time.

Between meetings of the governing body the chairman and the chief executive (or similar individual) should maintain regular contact particularly on matters affecting the charity's relations and reputation with the public. The chairman, as the representative of the governing body, may be called on to answer any questions resulting from reports in the press or the media about incidents involving the charity. Therefore it is vital that the chairman and the other honorary officers, if any (and if appropriate), should be kept informed of matters which are likely to attract public attention, favourable or otherwise. Similar considerations may apply to some extent to other trustees, for example those who may have special regional interests or responsibility.

Although trustees should be encouraged to take a wide interest in the operation of their charity they should be discouraged from giving instructions directly to employees without first consulting the chief executive or other senior member of staff responsible for that particular aspect of the charity's activity. Conversely, other than in exceptional circumstances staff should not lobby individual trustees. Staff with a grievance should use the charity's grievance procedure.

Ideally, individual trustees should not give instructions to members of staff unless authorised to do so by the governing body. An alternative approach on an important matter would be to inform the chairman or relevant honorary officer who would then raise the subject with the chief executive or other appropriate person. Any interference in matters of detail by trustees is likely to undermine the authority of those who carry out day-to-day management and administration. It may also have the effect of spreading confusion and uncertainty in the minds of employees who receive conflicting instructions from different sources. These principles also apply to those trustees who are members of any sub-committees. A new trustee should be advised as to how to deal with such situations; something which could be incorporated as part of an induction programme.

Division of responsibility for policy implementation

There are two important factors which affect the basic principle that it is the trustees as the governing body who are responsible for deciding policy and the staff (whether led by someone in the role of a chief executive or similar) who are responsible for the implementation of that policy.

First, it is necessary to draw a distinction between major policy decisions and those decisions which are made in carrying out policy. Decisions of policy can be made at different levels. A governing body may decide that as part of its strategy a particular service should be developed, for example by providing residential care or extending its provision. In reaching a decision of this kind it would be necessary to decide the allocation of the resources required, set priorities and establish criteria by which the feasibility of the project can be assessed and measured.

The chief executive, perhaps with the assistance of an ad hoc committee and technical staff, would formulate the detailed policy for the design and construction of any necessary accommodation and decide, for example, what equipment should be provided and how many should be employed to meet the criteria and 'make the project work'. It is important that guidelines should be established so that all of those involved are aware at which point in the hierarchy various decisions of policy are made.

Professional advice

The second factor is that the governing body will almost always require professional advice and assistance from the charity's staff or from outside advisers to ensure that a considered judgement is made in arriving at policy decisions. If the example of residential care is taken, then before devising its strategy the governing body should have sought professional advice about the project as well as the practicality of introducing what is proposed, taking account of the resources available and any statutory constraints that would restrict what could be done in practice and continue to be done over a sufficient period of time to justify the investment.

It is therefore important that the professional employees of a charity should be encouraged to participate fully in the formulation of policy as well as reporting back to the governing body on the progress of any project which the governing body has decided should be implemented. It follows that the chief executive, and in larger organisations other staff, for example senior managers dealing with finance or the provision of professional services, should attend the meetings of trustees.

In addition, if the trustees establish a committee to make decisions at the second level in the execution of its policy it is usually helpful, provided the charity's governing document permits, for senior management to become full members of the committee often (but sometimes confusingly) described as an executive or management committee. The proceedings of any such executive or management committee should always be reported back to the governing body so that it can be assured that decisions are being taken in line with the overall policy.

If the staff wish to comment adversely on policy or any of the conditions under which they are employed the correct line of communication must be observed and ideally it should be set out in a properly formulated grievance procedure contained in a contract of employment.

Employees and volunteers

The work which can be generally undertaken most easily by volunteers is where no particular or special training is required and only occasional involvement is needed; many fund-raising activities would fall into this category. A sponsored event which involves a specific programme, house-to-house collections, or other such fund-raising activities are good examples. Many such events can be and are, well-planned, organised and run by volunteers. However, as the charity grows there has to be some co-ordination to ensure that the fund-raising activities of independent groups of volunteers do not conflict. It may also be advisable to establish a framework in which such activities can be organised and conducted. For example, volunteer organisers may need guidelines to follow when hiring premises, or the charity may have its own logo or house style to be used in any displays and advertising.

Many large charities have their own fund-raising department employing staff who are responsible for issuing instructions and giving advice where appropriate, possibly working through the charity's regional employees who then have the task of helping local groups to recruit and advise volunteers about fund-raising.

There are similar considerations to be observed in the provision of local services by a charity. Such services can range from organising transport to operating local or neighbourhood centres. Employees will have the responsibility of co-ordinating the contributions of volunteers in a particular area so that the best use can be made of those resources. The amount of direct involvement by the charity's staff will depend on the nature of its activity and the skills which are available among its volunteers.

Any project which involves volunteers and employees is more likely to succeed where the volunteers appreciate that it is necessary for the charity to employ staff who can provide the continuity of effort and in some cases the necessary professional expertise which the volunteers may lack themselves. Problems can arise in situations where some volunteers have a particular enthusiasm and a deep and personal understanding of what the charity is established to achieve and yet the staff at times appear to be emotionally detached.

There are also a number of legal distinctions between volunteers and employees and these should always be borne in mind.

3.12 Specialist advisers and consultants

Requirement

An adviser is a person or organisation providing expertise which the charity requires and to which it does not otherwise have access. The adviser may be paid or unpaid, and if the latter the role would be honorary as mentioned in section 3.9.

Reasons for appointment

The use of advisers and consultants should not be regarded by the employees or volunteers as a reflection of their own ability or worth. For a charity to survive it must be run in a business-like and structured way and in law the trustees are required to use the same level of diligence and care as a prudent businessman would do in the management of his own business.

Purpose

It should be emphasised that the purpose of an adviser is to provide advice or a professional service. The function of an adviser is not to replace the management's responsibility to manage nor is it to undermine the trustees' responsibility for setting and monitoring the strategy of the charity.

An adviser's task is either to provide advice which is not available within the organisation or to supplement the existing expertise of the trustees, staff or volunteers.

Continuity of advisers

The charity may find that it needs some advisers on a permanent basis and others to meet specific or ad hoc requirements. For a charity which requires a solicitor or other similar adviser where knowledge and understanding of the charity are also important the adviser may be designated as the charity's appointed adviser and be so described in the charity's publications including its report and accounts. Quite often advice may be needed on minor matters from time to time which would normally be provided only by an adviser who is retained by the charity. Other advisers may be required to meet special circumstances, for example the evaluation and setting up of a new project or for raising the necessary finance.

Selection

There are two main criteria to be observed in selecting an adviser or consultant. The first is confidence in the ability of the adviser which can either be gained from the personal experience of someone connected with the charity, or as a result of general reputation. The second criteria is his appropriateness for the purpose required.

The level of the fees payable will probably be linked to the size and reputation of the adviser's organisation. It may therefore be inappropriate for a small or medium-sized charity to employ a national firm of accountants when a local firm could perhaps offer a less expensive and a more personal service. Any adviser though, should have particular experience in dealing with charity matters. It is common sense to invite two or three applicants or firms when a charity is seeking to appoint either a retained adviser or one for a specific purpose. Consequently each applicant should be given a specification in sufficient detail of what it is that the charity requires.

Retention

Periodically and at generally no less than five-year intervals the retention of advisers or a particular adviser should be considered on the basis of whether there remains a need for that adviser and/or whether the performance continues to be satisfactory. If, for example, a charity wishes to review the appointment of its insurance brokers the likelihood is that there would be a selection process every five years.

Categories

The number of advisers required is likely to be in inverse proportion to the number of employees. A charity of sufficient size will employ staff to deal with finance, legal matters, investment and property as well as the charity's own special field, for example the welfare of the aged or those suffering a particular physical disability. A solicitor may be required to advise on dealings with the Commission, or to provide legal services regarding the charity's property or contracts of employment as well as any other legal areas relevant to the charity.

The following are examples of specialist advisers a charity may require:

- ☐ Computer consultant.
- ☐ Fund-raiser.
- ☐ Insurance broker.
- ☐ Investment adviser.
- ☐ Marketing consultant.
- ☐ Property adviser.
- ☐ Property surveyor.
- ☐ Publicity adviser.
- ☐ Solicitor.
- ☐ Specialist advice relevant to the field in which the charity operates, for example a medical adviser.

3.13 Draft letters to be sent to a trustee or director/trustee on appointment

Draft letter to a new trustee of an unincorporated charitable association

Dear

Your appointment as trustee

Following your appointment today as a trustee of this charity, I thought that it would be useful if I were to set out a number of matters which I hope you will find helpful.

Although I know you have seen the charity's governing document you should have your own copy to retain, and this is enclosed. I also enclose a schedule setting out the dates of the [council] [management or executive committee] meetings for the rest of this calendar year together with details of the basis on which you may claim expenses for attendance. An agenda with supporting papers is circulated approximately a week before each meeting.

In addition to the specific duties imposed on a trustee by the Charities Act 1993 you are under a general duty to act in good faith and to exercise your powers for the benefit of the charity as a whole. Consequently your personal interests should not be allowed to conflict with your overriding duty to act at all times for the sole benefit of the charity.

You will note from clause [   ] of the governing document that all trustees retire at each AGM and are eligible for re-election. If you require any information concerning the charity and I am unable to provide it then I will endeavour to let you know where it can be obtained. A copy of the charity's 'boardroom practice' code is also enclosed.

If you wish to call a meeting of the trustees to discuss a matter which cannot wait until the next scheduled meeting, you should contact the chairman, but at the same time would you please let me know that you are doing so.

Yours sincerely

Secretary

Draft letter to a new director/trustee of a charitable company

Dear

Your appointment as director/trustee

Following your appointment today as a director/trustee of this charitable company, I thought that it would be useful if I were to set out a number of matters which I hope you will find helpful.

Although I know you have seen a copy of the company's memorandum and articles and association, you should have your own copy to retain and this is enclosed. You will note in particular that as a director/trustee you will [be required to retire annually although continue to be eligible for re-election] [in accordance with article   be required] [not be required] to retire by rotation].

I enclose a schedule setting out the dates of board meetings for the rest of this calendar year together with details of the basis on which you may claim expenses for attendance. An agenda with supporting papers is circulated approximately a week before each meeting.

In order that I can notify Companies House of your appointment will you please let me know your forenames and, if appropriate, any previous forenames or surnames. I have taken it that your nationality is British and that your business occupation is that of a [   ]. If you have any other directorships would you please let me have details of the companies concerned. Will you please also let me know your date of birth as this must be notified to Companies House.

In addition to the duties and responsibilities of a charity trustee and the specific duties imposed on director/trustees by the Companies Acts 1985–89 and related legislation, director/trustees are under a fiduciary duty to act in good faith and to exercise their powers for the benefit of the company as a whole. Consequently a director/trustee's personal interests must not be allowed to conflict with his overriding duty to act at all times for the sole benefit of the company.

If you require any information concerning the company you should contact me, and if I am unable to provide it I will endeavour to let you know where it can be obtained. A copy of the company's 'boardroom practice' code is also enclosed.

If you wish to call a board meeting of the director/trustees to discuss a matter which cannot wait until the next scheduled meeting you should contact the chairman, but at the same time would you please let me know that you are doing so.

Yours sincerely

Secretary

3.14 Other useful publications

Palmer, P. and Harrow, J. *Rethinking Charity Trusteeship* (1994) ICSA Publishing.

The Charity Commission publishes:

CC3	Responsibilities of Charity Trustees
CC3(a)	Responsibilities of Charity Trustees – a summary
CC9	Political Activities and Campaigning by Charities
CC11	Remuneration of Charity Trustees
CC36	Making a Scheme
CC44	Small Charities: Alteration of Trusts, Transfer of Property, Expenditure of Capital
CC49	Charities and Insurance

NCVO publishes:

Trustee Liability Insurance
The Good Trustee Guide

4

COMMITTEE ADMINISTRATION

4.1 The need for committees

Rationale

Many organisations, particularly those in the voluntary sector, find it necessary to establish committees and sub-committees for a variety of reasons.

The decision-making process often has to be shared because the subject matter is too complex or time consuming for one individual to deal with alone. It may also be preferable for decisions to be taken and be seen to be taken as a result of a broadly based discussion rather than by one or two individuals imposing their own views.

In this chapter the term 'committee' also includes a sub-committee.

Specific purposes for which a committee may be established

One such purpose would be to co-ordinate a particular part of the work of the charity – a fund-raising campaign is a good example, or to establish and manage a specific project, perhaps the building of new premises. A committee may also be established to carry out an advisory role with regard to technical matters or be given a remit which is purely consultative in order to obtain the views and opinions of various individuals who have particular knowledge of the subject matter. In this way any conclusions which are reached not only represent the views of the majority but are informed decisions as well.

It may also be advisable to establish a committee to make recommendations on matters which are fairly complex or specialised and which would make detailed consideration by the governing body very difficult and, more to the point, could take too long.

Functional committees

The governing body of a charity can, if its constitution allows, delegate some of its work to a committee, typically a management or executive committee which will manage the day-to-day activities of the charity. It will depend on the size and complexity of the charity whether such a committee is able to discharge all the functional responsibilities.

In the larger and more complex organisation the executive or management committee (however described) may itself delegate some of its work on particular matters, for example property, to a separate functional sub-committee which may also have management and advisory responsibilities. An advisory committee may in some instances be given limited powers to make decisions – perhaps to approve a limited range of payments to applicant beneficiaries.

4.2 The role of the governing body

Constitution

The governing document should specify how the governing body is constituted and how members may be appointed to it or retire or be removed from it. Reference should be made to the model draft constitutions in Appendices 1 and 2. As already mentioned the governing body has the responsibility for setting the strategy and monitoring the success or otherwise in achieving the charity's objects. The governing document should also set out the powers and duties of the governing body, although some governing documents are vague or imprecise in this respect and do cause problems for the trustees of such charities – hence the need to review and overhaul the governing document from time to time.

The governing body of a charitable trust or a charitable association is its trustees and the governing body of a charitable company is the board of directors/trustees.

The variety of descriptions which are applied to a governing body can be confusing. The governing document of a charitable association may not refer to the term trustee at all and instead describe the trustees, for example, as the executive committee. The board of director/trustees is often described in the articles of association as the council of management or as in Appendix 2, the management committee. On the other hand the term executive or management committee can be and often is used to describe a functional committee appointed by the governing body to carry out certain aspects of the charity's work generally on a day-to-day basis. It is necessary therefore to distinguish between these terms when they are being used in different ways.

Decision-making process

How decisions are made will depend in part on the size and complexity of the charity's organisation and structure. It may be that the governing body takes every decision and also carries out an executive role in managing the affairs of the charity on a day-to-day basis. In other cases the governing body will not perform an executive role itself but will appoint a management or executive committee which is subject to control by the governing body.

Monitoring by the governing body

The governing body has to monitor the effects, both positive and negative, of its policy-making and ensure that its decisions are implemented so far as is practicable, given time and financial constraints. To a greater or lesser extent it is the responsibility of the secretary to facilitate and check the way in which policy is implemented, although in small charities the governing body itself will almost inevitably do this.

The governing body of a large charity will meet its obligation to supervise by considering reports or reviewing the minutes of any committee which it has established.

4.3 Terms of reference

It is the responsibility of the governing body to define the purpose for which a committee is established and to specify how such purpose is to be achieved. The extent of any authority which is delegated must be clearly stated, as should the procedure to be followed in reporting back to the governing body. Specific terms of reference should be drawn up by the secretary in consultation with the chairman of the charity or voluntary organisation so that a draft of the terms of reference can be presented to the governing body for approval.

It should also be clearly stated whether the purpose for which the committee is established is executive or advisory, and stipulating those decisions which it is entitled to act upon itself and which decisions must be referred back to the governing body. Where a committee has been given executive powers, any financial limits must be quantified.

The governing body should also agree the maximum and minimum number of members required to form a committee, and it may also be appropriate to specify the kind of experience which is required of its members. The frequency of meetings should be agreed, as should the number of members required to constitute a quorum.

4.4 Composition of committees

Appointment of chairman and other officers

The governing body would normally appoint a committee chairman whose main role would be to ensure that the committee discharges its responsibilities properly and in a timely way. A vice-chairman should also be appointed if appropriate.

The chairman should have sufficient knowledge of committee procedure and ideally combine this with the ability to control proceedings without being too confrontational – attributes which are partly inherent and partly gained through experience. The vice-chairman, who may be appointed by the committee itself, should be able to preside at meetings in the chairman's absence and also to assist him in dealing with the business of the committee between meetings.

The secretary of the committee will usually be the secretary of the charity or voluntary organisation, an arrangement which also assists in promoting good communication between the governing body and its committees, whose activities will almost certainly be interdependent.

Selection of committee members

The committee may consist entirely of members of the governing body or comprise some members from the governing body and others who may be selected from members of staff, supporters or members of the charity with particular experience of the subject matter.

The role of staff employed by the larger charity

It is advisable in the case of a larger charity for a member of staff to be in attendance at all meetings of the governing body and any committee. It may be that an employee is a member of, for example, the management or executive committee in his own right, in which case he will be entitled to vote and take part in making decisions. If several employees are members of a committee the voting rules should preclude the possibility of the employees forming a majority for voting purposes.

Legal aspects

In determining the composition of a committee any legal requirements must be observed. The governing document of a charity should, as already mentioned, preferably specify the minimum and maximum number of members of any committee. It is also important to ensure that a quorum is present at any committee meeting which is held. Depending on the circumstances it may also be appropriate to specify the period of notice to be given to members.

Scope and spread of representation

As a general rule the governing body will need more members than a specialist or functional committee because the work of the latter is usually more specific. The scope of representation can also influence the composition of the committee if it is considered advisable to include members who have different backgrounds and skills which are complementary.

Quorum and ability to attend meetings

The governing document of a charity or the terms of reference of a committee will specify the number of members who are to constitute a quorum, but against that must be balanced the practical difficulty of ensuring that sufficient committee members are able to attend meetings regularly. If a committee is fairly small it may be appropriate that the quorum should be all the members who have been appointed.

The efficient conduct of business

If a committee is too large there is the likelihood that many points of view will be expressed with the result that it may be difficult to reach any conclusions or decisions. The number of persons appointed to a committee must be manageable and not so many as to make its proceedings unwieldy and too lengthy. It is, however, difficult to be specific about the optimum size of the committee because all charities and their 'modus operandi' are different. What may suit one may not necessarily suit another.

Too many committees!

There is a danger in creating too many sub-committees because this could lead, among other things, to a lack of control or difficulties in communication as borne out by the Charity Commission report regarding the Royal British Legion. There is also the risk that the existence of a number of sub-committees will take up a disproportionate share of the resources of the charity.

5

GOVERNANCE

5.1 The status, authority and liability of the secretary of a charitable company

Common law principles

How does the status and authority of a secretary of a charitable company differ from that of a secretary of an unincorporated charity? In many respects the position of the secretary of a charitable company is more clearly defined, although it would not be difficult to argue by extension that some of the general common law principles, i.e. court decisions, would also apply to the secretary of an unincorporated charity or for that matter other voluntary or not-for-profit organisations.

The status of the company secretary

The status of the secretary of a limited company which includes all charitable companies limited by guarantee has gradually developed over the past century and continues to do so. In 1887 a judge commented that 'a company secretary is a mere servant; his position is that he is to do what he is told, and no person can assume that he has any authority to represent anything at all; nor can anyone assume that statements made by him are to be accepted as trustworthy without further inquiry.' Even in 1902 the duties of a company secretary were described as 'of a limited and of a somewhat humble character'.

The extent to which the company secretary's responsibilities have developed in the meantime has been confirmed by successive Companies Acts which require that every limited company including a company limited by guarantee must appoint a secretary. It should be noted that there is a distinction to be drawn between the role of a director (which includes of course a director/trustee) and the secretary because a sole director of a company cannot also be its secretary.

The 1985 Companies Act also provides that anything to be done or authorised by or to the secretary may be done by or to an assistant secretary. However, if there is no assistant or deputy capable of acting the board may authorise any director of the company to act as the secretary, unless of course that director is the sole director of the company. Provided therefore that a director is not the sole director of the company there is nothing to prevent a director undertaking the required action, for example, by attesting the company's seal if it has one.

The Panorama case

In the Court of Appeal in 1971 in the case of *Panorama Developments (Guildford)* v. *Fidelis Furnishing Fabrics Ltd* it was recognised that the company secretary by virtue of that office has ostensible authority to enter into certain contracts on behalf of a company. The company secretary was described in the Panorama case by one of the judges as 'the chief administrative officer of the company' and by another judge as 'an officer of the company with extensive duties and responsibilities'. These statements represent a somewhat different interpretation from those made about the position of the company secretary in 1887 and 1902.

The point that had to be decided in the Panorama case was whether the authority of the secretary was sufficient for him to be able to enter into some kinds of contracts on behalf of the company. The secretary would only have had such authority if it had been specifically granted by the board of directors or by the inference which arises from the importance of his status in the company, which is known as 'ostensible authority'. The court held that the company secretary did have such ostensible authority in certain circumstances.

In the case of a charitable company which is *not* a company established to carry out a commercial purpose it could be said to follow that the ostensible authority of the secretary is sufficiently wide ranging to embrace virtually every aspect of administration and management. The same could not perhaps be said of the secretary of a charity trading company which has a quasi-commercial character and purpose and the probability therefore is that the authority of the secretary of such a company would be more restricted to such things as hiring cars or buying stationery – in other words in line with the 1971 Panorama case.

The point to be emphasised is that the law is still in a state of evolution and will no doubt be so for some time to come, particularly when looked at in the context of the difficulties there are in defining the role of the director/trustees of a charitable company compared with that of employees who are responsible for the day-to-day management of the charity's activities. To some extent the concept of the ostensible authority of the secretary of a charitable company should be of more concern to the director/trustees who may find their charitable company bound by the unauthorised action of the secretary with perhaps expensive or unforeseen consequences.

The Companies Acts do not define the duties of the company secretary in detail or, for example, state specifically that he should maintain the registers of members or director/trustees or send the statutory returns to the Registrar of Companies. However, the majority of forms prescribed under the Companies Acts provide in most instances for signature by a director *or* the secretary. A company's annual return is a good example.

Although it is a requirement that all limited companies appoint a company secretary there is no direct penalty for failing to do so.

The potential liability of the secretary of a charitable company under companies legislation

The company secretary is an officer of the company by virtue of the 1985 Companies Act and as already mentioned he can incur personal liability if in breach of the many requirements imposed by companies legislation. Consequently the secretary of a charitable company can incur a financial penalty or exceptionally have imposed a term of imprisonment if prosecuted. However, s. 727 of the 1985 Act does enable the court to grant relief in any proceedings taken against a company secretary as an officer of the company if it appears to the court that such an individual although liable because of negligence, default, breach of duty or of trust acted honestly and reasonably and ought fairly to be excused having regard to all the circumstances.

The clear advice is that such dispensation should not be relied upon. The problem should be avoided by maintaining proper control over the way in which the charitable company operates and is managed.

The potential liability of the company secretary for negligence

Additionally, the company secretary may be liable to a claim for damages and compensation by the company if he is negligent. This is not external liability for a breach of companies legislation but the liability of the company secretary to the company because he is in breach of his contractual duties and responsibilities to the company. It should be noted by virtue of the 1985 Act that any attempt to exempt a director, manager or any other officer (which would include the company secretary) or employee of a company in respect of negligence, default, breach of duty or of trust is void even if the indemnity is in writing or there is such a provision in the articles of association.

It is worth noting that s. 61 of the Trustee Act 1925 states 'that if it appears to the court that a *trustee* is or may be personally liable for any breach of trust but has acted honestly or reasonably and ought fairly to be excused the court may relieve him either wholly or partly from personal liability for the same'. This section refers only to a breach of trust by a trustee (which includes a director/trustee) but not the secretary.

5.2 Good 'boardroom' practice – a code for trustees and charity secretaries

Written procedures and guidelines

The trustees should establish written procedures and guidelines for the conduct of their business. A copy of these written procedures should be given to each trustee on appointment. Compliance should be monitored perhaps by a committee of trustees, and any breach of procedure should be reported to the governing body as a whole.

The secretary should ensure that each trustee is given on appointment sufficient information to enable him to carry out his duties. In particular guidance should cover the procedures:

☐ for obtaining information concerning the charity or charitable company;
☐ for requisitioning a meeting of trustees or director/trustees.

The draft letters in section 3.13 which it is recommended should be sent to newly appointed trustees include both of these matters.

Provision of information and 'material' contracts

In the conduct of the charity's business there are two fundamental concepts which should be observed: first, that each trustee or director/trustee should receive the same information at the same time and secondly, that each trustee or director/trustee should be given sufficient time in which to consider such information.

The trustees should identify those matters which require their prior approval and lay down procedures to be followed when exceptionally a decision is required before the next meeting of trustees on any matter not required by law to be considered by the trustees as a whole. All material contracts and especially those not in the ordinary course of a charity's activities should as a matter of basic principle be referred to the trustees for a decision prior to the charity or charitable company entering into any commitment.

The trustees should approve beforehand what in their view would constitute a contract which was 'material' and 'not in the ordinary course of the charity's activities'. These definitions should be brought to the attention of anyone who should be informed, for example a member of staff who has responsibility for negotiating contracts. Where there is any uncertainty regarding the materiality or nature of any proposed contract it should normally be considered by the governing body as a whole.

Agenda setting and minutes

Decisions regarding which items should appear on the agenda for a meeting of trustees and the presentation of such items should be made by the chairman in consultation with the secretary. The secretary must be entitled to be present at all trustee meetings and be responsible for the preparation of the minutes of such meetings. The minutes should record the decisions taken and provide sufficient background. All papers presented at a meeting of trustees should be clearly identified in the minutes and retained for reference. Procedures should be established for the approval and circulation of minutes of meetings.

5.3 Principles of good governance

Implications for the relationship between trustees and management

The relationship between the governing body and the management team of a charity or charitable company raises a number of issues. One view is that the governing body should only determine overall direction and strategy and set desired targets and not get 'bogged down' in the details. In the same way as happens in the commercial world the trustees or director/trustees should set medium and long-term goals for their charity as well as an annual bottom line. Trustees and director/trustees should look more at enabling staff to solve problems rather than giving staff detailed instructions as to how they should proceed.

Another question to be resolved is the selection of trustees, something which was considered in Chapter 3. Should trustees be selected through a democratic representative process or should they be recruited in response to the skill-mix requirements of a charity which would make its body of trustees more effective? If so, selection might be better done through a formal recruitment process which seems increasingly to be the way.

A separate category of trustee is the representative trustee who has been nominated by an organisation involved with the charity or charitable company. The problem which can occur with a representative trustee is that he may not always appreciate the possibility that a conflict of interest can arise. The overriding duty of any charity trustee is to look after the interests of the charity of which he is a trustee and not the interests of the sponsoring organisation which nominated him.

Cadbury recommendations

Ever since the creation of the Cadbury committee governance has by extension become part of the 'conventional wisdom' among commentators and those involved with charities and voluntary organisations.

What exactly does governance mean? The fact that the question even has to be asked implies some doubt as to its precise meaning. There is also the wider question, which is to what extent does good governance in the commercial sector have any relevance to charitable or voluntary organisations? Clearly there is a striking distinction between the commercial and the not-for-profit sectors, although this distinction may be less clear-cut than it used to be.

There are a number of reasons why standards of corporate governance in the commercial world fell and have not been entirely retrieved despite Cadbury and subsequently Hampel. One reason is the belief that it is imperative that commercial companies should maintain their independence. The quest for independence is not so much a problem in the charitable sector. There are some charity trustees who would not be unhappy if their own charity did lose its independence and amalgamate with another in what is becoming a more hostile environment.

Boards of directors of commercial companies on the other hand, particularly Stock Exchange listed companies are usually looking over their shoulders for the next predator, real or imagined. The temptation therefore to keep the share price high is almost irresistible and the methods which are sometimes deployed are questionable despite the best efforts of the regulatory authorities and the law. It is perhaps the case, although some would disagree, that the pressure on charities to carry out financial window-dressing is not so acute, although even that may be changing.

Charities should do their utmost to maintain transparency in the way in which they conduct themselves in order to attract the funds on which their very survival depends and to retain suitable people as employees. It does not take much for the press to seize on misbehaviour by a charity or charity trustees and to report it with zeal. In 1992 the Commission had to intervene in the management of the Royal British Legion because of the failure of that organisation to set up an appropriate management structure to deal with a new venture where there was a degree of commercial risk. There have been a number of other widely reported examples in recent years and the trend seems to be growing.

Other issues

There are other governance issues to be addressed, one of which is the vexed question of whether or not charity trustees should be remunerated, a topic dealt with in section 3.7. Should director/trustees ever by allowed to have an interest, however remote, in any contract with their charitable company? On the other side of the coin there is the debate as to whether the salaries received by some chief executives and other senior personnel employed by charities are too high.

So against this background, which is ever changing, the question to be asked is: What can the individual charity secretary do to introduce and maintain the appropriate standards of governance? Does the charity secretary's position lend itself to this role and what is the status and authority of the secretary which will enable him to discharge such a responsibility? The core duties which were outlined in Chapter 1 do put the charity secretary at the heart of his charity's organisation and 'being' and therefore he is perhaps in as good a position as anyone to take responsibility for implementing and monitoring proper standards of governance. Occasionally it will be necessary for him to show firmness and to say and do what he knows is right despite criticism, discontent and even the open hostility of some trustees, as well as perhaps other colleagues within the organisation.

Important in all of this is the attitude of the chairman. The chairman of a charity fulfils a particularly influential role because he can have a significant bearing on the way in which the charity views its obligation to maintain ethical and appropriate standards of governance. Another relevant factor is the field of activity in which the charity operates; a social campaigning charity may have a different approach than would a charity which looks after the spiritual interests of seafarers. Grant-making charities are of course in a different category altogether.

If there is any political in-fighting between the chairman and, say, the chief executive this will have consequences for the way in which the governance of that charity is perceived, not only by the staff but by a wider audience as well. It may be that the charity secretary needs greater protection (even though, all other things being equal, compensation would normally be payable in the event of unfair dismissal) and that he should not be subject to the threat of summary dismissal for putting forward a point of view which may be unpalatable.

5.4   Other useful publications

Hind, A. *The Governance and Management of Charities* (1995) Voluntary Sector Press.

NCVO publishes:

The Good Trustee Guide

6

CONSTITUTIONS AND GOVERNING DOCUMENTS

6.1　Incorporation – advantages and disadvantages

Advantages

It sometimes comes as a surprise to the trustees of unincorporated charities to learn that they can be made personally responsible for the debts and other liabilities of their charity if it has insufficient resources to meet the legitimate claims of third parties.

The following are the main advantages for the trustees of a charity to achieve its purpose constituted as a charitable company:

- [ ] A charitable company is a separate legal entity distinct from its members and director/trustees and can therefore carry out its purpose and objects in its own name.
- [ ] A charitable company has perpetual succession unless it is wound up or struck off the register by the Registrar of Companies. This means that a charitable company's continuing existence is not immediately affected by death, bankruptcy or retirement of any of its members or director/trustees.
- [ ] The debts incurred and contracts entered into by a charitable company are the responsibility of the company and not its members or director/trustees. The only liability of a member is to contribute a specified amount of money if the company is wound up and there are insufficient assets to meet the claims of creditors.
- [ ] The property of a charitable company belongs to and is vested in the company so that there is no change in the legal ownership of the property when a member leaves or a director/trustee retires. In contrast, where the trustees of an unincorporated charity hold property on its behalf and a trustee retires there has to be a transfer of the formal legal title of the property to include an incoming trustee, assuming there is one. This involves expense and is an administrative inconvenience.

Disadvantages

There are some disadvantages which include:

- The additional cost of keeping a charitable company in existence, although this is not generally excessive.
- In addition to the potential liability of the secretary and for that matter the director/trustees, as officers of a charitable company arising from a breach of company law, there are many more requirements imposed by company law to be met by a charitable company compared with an unincorporated charity, although the differences are to some extent beginning to narrow.

6.2 The unincorporated charity's constitution

Outline framework of a typical unincorporated charity's constitution

Every unincorporated charity should preferably have a written constitution, either in the form of a trust deed, or in the case of a charitable association a governing document which sets out among other things:

- The name of the charity.
- Its purpose and objectives.
- Powers (including investment powers).
- How its membership is defined.
- The rules relating to the way the general meetings of members are held.
- The composition of the governing body (council, council or committee of management or executive committee).
- The procedures to be followed by the governing body and any of its committees or sub-committees.
- The way in which nominations are to be made for appointment to the governing body or other committee(s).
- Provisions relating to finance and property.
- How the governing document can be amended.
- How the assets should be applied if the charity is dissolved.

Ensuring compliance with the trust deed or governing document

One of the fundamental responsibilities of the charity secretary is to make certain that the governing document is observed in all respects and that the purpose and objects of the charity are not exceeded or ignored. If the trustees of a charity want to do something which its governing document does not permit then it may be necessary for the trustees to apply to the Commission requesting it to make a formal scheme to broaden or extend the objects of the charity.

Points to check in a review of the governing document

Although there has to be compliance with an unincorporated charity's governing document, nonetheless it does not mean that it is incapable of amendment or is written on 'tablets of stone'. The secretary, with the trustees, should from time to time review the provisions of the governing document of their charity to examine whether or not its objects can be achieved in a more appropriate or efficient manner, or whether the rules which regulate the day-to-day running and management of the charity should be changed or amplified. One particular aspect to check is the way in which membership of the charity is defined: Who precisely is entitled to attend and vote at general meetings?

If the charity is established by trust deed there is less of a problem because the trustees are usually the only members with voting rights. This is not necessarily so in the case of a more broadly based charitable association with an elected committee and a number of members. For example if the governing document of a charitable association provides that membership is available to anyone (individual or organisation) who wishes to support it and who completes the prescribed application form, only those who have complied with this requirement will be the properly constituted members. In other words the mere fact that an individual has made a donation to the charity or is a volunteer does not mean he is automatically a member with voting rights if the membership admission procedures stipulated in the constitution have not been satisfied.

Continuing membership is sometimes dependent on payment of an annual subscription. If a member fails to pay the subscription, then, depending on the precise wording of the governing document, his membership may lapse – see clause 6 of Appendix 1. If membership does lapse it will mean that he is no longer entitled to participate as a member and therefore would not be able to attend and vote at general meetings.

The governing document of a charitable association should specifically provide for the establishment of sub-committees, either executive or functional and state on what basis the proceedings of such sub-committees are to be regulated, how the appointment of members is to be made, and any limitations on the decisions a sub-committee can make. Can the trustees themselves be members of a sub-committee? It is usual for some of them to be so but the governing document should expressly make the position clear.

Consent of the Commission to proposed amendments to a charity's governing document

If the governing document does not contain a power of amendment or if the power is not sufficient to allow the kind of changes the trustees believe necessary and they wish to hold to that view there are two alternative procedures which can be followed depending on the level of the charity's annual income and how it is constituted.

If the annual income of the charity (which is neither an exempt charity nor a charitable company) is less than £5,000 the trustees may exercise the power contained in the 1993 Act to pass a resolution, requiring a two-thirds majority, to modify or replace the objects of the charity or any administrative provisions. A copy of the resolution must be sent to the Commission and its consent obtained before any changes can be implemented. The trustees are also required to advertise their proposals and consult the public, although the means by which they carry out these requirements are for the trustees to decide as they think is reasonable in the circumstances. Any additional objects must, however be similar to the original objects, or an extension of them. The Charity Commission has published leaflet CC44 which deals with this topic.

In the case of a charity with an annual income of more than £5,000 it will be necessary to apply to the Commission for a scheme to modify, amend or replace the existing governing document. The procedure is fairly complicated and legal advice should be obtained, or assistance sought from the Commission itself – see leaflet CC36.

6.3 The charitable company's constitution

Memorandum

Every charitable company (as with all other limited companies) will have a set of memorandum and articles of association. The memorandum contains the name of the company, its objects and the way in which these are to be achieved or enhanced (usually referred to as ancillary powers), a statement that the liability of the members is limited, and a guarantee which sets out how much each member is to contribute to the company in the event that it is wound up and the assets are insufficient to meet its liabilities.

There must also be a clause stating how any surplus should be distributed on a winding up. In many ways a member of a charitable company is similar to the shareholder of a company limited by shares although a member of a charitable company is not entitled to participate in any surplus revenue as a dividend or a share of the assets on a winding up.

The articles of association

The articles are more detailed and set out the rules by which the company is to be administered. There will be included, for example, a definition of the members, how they become members and how such membership may be terminated. There will be provisions dealing with how general meetings are held, how often, on what basis they should be convened, and how their proceedings are to be conducted. There will also be provisions dealing with the constitution of the board of director/trustees – which may also be described (sometimes confusingly) as a council of management, executive committee, or as in Appendix 2 management committee – and how the proceedings of such a body are to be conducted and regulated.

The governing body, however described, is the board of director/trustees, i.e. those persons who have the responsibility for ensuring that the charitable company achieves its purposes and objects prudently and within the law. Other provisions include the basis on which a member may appoint a proxy (although a number of charitable companies do not allow the appointment of proxies), and the periodic retirement or rotation of the director/trustees.

It is clearly important that the secretary acquires a detailed knowledge of the contents of the memorandum and articles of association in order to ensure that no breaches occur.

Ensuring compliance with the memorandum and articles of association

In the same way as it is important that the governing document of an unincorporated charity should be followed in all respects, so it is with a charitable company. Failure to do so may invalidate decisions reached either by the director/trustees or members of a charitable company in general meetings, and either outcome must be avoided. If the charitable company were to depart from its charitable objects and loss resulted, the director/trustees may be made personally liable for such breach in the same way as the trustees of an unincorporated charity are liable if they commit a breach of trust. Limited liability in this instance is of no avail!

Points to check in review of memorandum and articles of association

Broadly similar considerations apply as those discussed in relation to an unincorporated charity. The secretary of a charitable company should be mindful of the need to review periodically the contents of the memorandum and articles which particularly in many old established charitable companies may not have kept pace with changes in legislation and developments in practice and procedure. Many have a distinctly nineteenth-century flavour.

A charitable company, like any other company, must have members who can clearly be shown as such for the purpose of passing resolutions at general meetings. The articles of charitable companies often contain archaic and anachronistic rules defining their membership. Many of those associated with the charitable company in some way will regard themselves automatically as members of the company, but they would not be so if the correct procedure leading to membership has not been followed. Indeed it would often be quite inappropriate for all those associated with the charitable company to be members; the practical problems and cost of holding formal general meetings with many thousands of members with voting rights would be considerable – although the National Trust does manage to do it very well, but presumably at no little cost!

The question to be considered is: Can it be said with absolute certainty who are the members of a charitable company with voting rights and therefore liable to contribute if required under the terms of the guarantee in the event of an insolvent winding up? Nor does it follow that the director/trustees of a charitable company are members unless they have specifically complied with the rules set out in the articles of association defining the means by which membership is attained.

The articles of association should specifically provide for the establishment of sub-committees and state on what basis the proceedings of such sub-committees are to be regulated. Are the provisions in the articles relating to the proceedings of general meetings of members logical, or should they be reviewed to reflect what actually happens or ideally should happen in practice?

It is advisable to carry out such a review before a problem arises, and although not every problem can be anticipated a number of the more obvious ones can and should be avoided. It must never be forgotten that a simple majority of the members of the charitable company attending and voting at a general meeting have the power to dismiss the director/trustees. Although it is unlikely to happen it is nonetheless a possibility.

Consent of Commission to proposed amendments

Since 1 January 1993 any charitable company wishing to alter its objects or any other provision in its memorandum or articles of association relating to the way in which the company's assets and property may be applied must first obtain the written consent of the Commission to the alterations. Consent must be obtained before the special resolution of the members of a charitable company is passed, and any purported alteration made without the Commission's prior written consent will not be valid. It is important to understand therefore that the consent of the Commission cannot be obtained retrospectively.

In the event of an authorised and therefore valid change, copies of the special resolution effecting the alteration, the amended memorandum and articles of association, and the Commission's consent must also be filed with the Registrar of Companies.

6.4 Other useful publications

The Charity Commission publishes:

CC36   Making a Scheme
CC44   Small Charities: Alteration of Trusts, Transfer of Property, Expenditure of Capital

7

MEETINGS

7.1 Frequency and timing

Schedule of meetings

It is important to decide how frequently meetings should be held and their timing. If practicable it would be sensible to decide a programme of the meetings of a standing committee for the ensuing year so that all its members are aware of the dates well in advance. Even where a committee is not required to meet at regular intervals it is advisable that at each meeting the date for the next meeting is agreed.

The extent, type and volume of work

The governing body which has to establish and monitor policy will probably need to meet less frequently than a committee with responsibility for a specific function which is ongoing, for example the control of finance. The governing body may only meet a few times a year, perhaps every three months, but a finance committee will have to meet more often. Where the workload of a committee increases it may be preferable for meetings to be held more frequently rather than to increase their length.

Availability of committee members

If the frequency of meetings is increased some members may find it difficult to attend, with the result that they may decide that they cannot continue which, depending on their experience, could be a considerable loss to the organisation.

Amount of work likely to be carried out between meetings

Once a committee has made its decisions it may be necessary for some of its members to carry out various tasks and report back to the next meeting.

Consequently there must be sufficient time to allow for such work to be undertaken and reviewed by the chairman and perhaps the secretary. The problem, however, is to assess how long such a process will actually take.

Staff availability and use of resources

A balance has to be struck between the time which employees or volunteers can spend in attending meetings and the time which they should devote to the charity's other work. This should be taken into account so that their contribution is commensurate with the efficient use of limited resources.

Timing of meetings

This depends on a number of factors. A finance committee, for example, will require monthly financial reports several days ahead of each meeting, and a fund-raising committee will need details of proposed fund-raising activities for perhaps a year ahead. The availability of such information will clearly have an influence on the timing of their respective meetings. It is also necessary to decide on which day of the week the meeting will take place and when it is to commence. This may result in evening meetings occasionally being held in order to ensure optimum attendance by members.

7.2 The law

General rules

Most, if not all, human activity is regulated by the law – even meetings. The law of meetings as it affects a charity depends to some extent on whether the charity is unincorporated or is a charitable company. There are common law rules which apply to all meetings generally (including those of charities) and additional specific rules which apply to charitable companies.

A charitable company's articles of association will almost invariably incorporate the regulations which are to be followed at meetings of the members of the company, and to some extent meetings of the director/trustees, and of any committees.

The governing document of a charitable unincorporated association

The governing document will prescribe the frequency at which general meetings of members are to be held and may even set out the business to be transacted at the annual general meeting; for an example see clause 10 of

Appendix 1. There will also be provisions relating to other meetings of members, sometimes called special meetings. The role of the chairman may also be specified. There will also be rules detailing the composition of the management or executive committee, the procedures that such a committee must adopt and how its members are to be appointed.

The governing document of a charitable company

The governing document of a charitable company as already noted is its memorandum and articles of association. The articles set out the rules regulating how proceedings at general meetings are to be conducted, how the votes of members will be taken, how and to what extent the powers and duties of the director/trustees are defined, whether the director/trustees are to retire periodically and the manner in which their proceedings are to be conducted including whether or not the chairman is to have a casting vote.

General requirements

The main requirements to be observed are that meetings should be properly convened and that a quorum is present. Any meeting which is held must also comply with the more detailed rules contained in an unincorporated charity's governing document or the articles of association of a charitable company.

Notices of meetings

The Charities Act 1993 provides that any notices which are required or authorised by the trusts of the charity (in other words the governing document) to be given to a charity trustee, member or subscriber may be sent by post to any address which has been given by the individual and recorded in the list of charity trustees, members or subscribers for the time being in use at the office or the principal office of the charity. Where any such notice is sent by post it is deemed to have been given by the time the letter containing it would be delivered in the ordinary course of post. No notice required to be given of any meeting or election need be given to any charity trustee, member or subscriber if the list does not give an address in the UK.

Length of notice

Where a period of notice refers to 'clear days' it excludes the day on which the notice is deemed to have been sent and the day of the meeting itself. It is also necessary to give notice of any meeting of a charitable company so as to comply with any requirements contained in the articles of association and in companies legislation. Failure to do so may invalidate a meeting. Reference is also made to this topic in section 7.5.

7.3 Administration of meetings

Secretarial support

The level of support will vary depending on the type of meeting and who is available to act as its secretary. The secretary of a large charity should attend all meetings and may be assisted by another member of staff.

In some cases one individual may be responsible for providing secretarial support to several committees under the guidance and supervision of the secretary. If the charity has a substantial number of committees it will be necessary to arrange for the production and distribution of agendas and previous minutes and to prepare other papers as well as dealing with correspondence.

The secretary's role before a meeting

Prior to a meeting it will be necessary for the secretary to:

- Ensure the availability of the venue and depending on the duration of the meeting, refreshments.
- prepare the agenda in conjunction with the chairman and if appropriate the chief executive.
- Review with the chairman the way in which the business of the meeting will be conducted in order to make sure that the chairman and members have the requisite information to make it effective.
- Arrange for the agenda with the supporting papers and financial reports to be distributed at least a week beforehand so that the members have sufficient time in which to consider any items for discussion.
- Remind anyone who will be presenting information or reporting to the meeting.
- Make sure that a quorum will be present and not leave it until the last moment.
- Remind any external consultant or adviser who is to attend that the meeting is taking place.

The agenda

The format of an agenda should be along the following lines subject to variations to suit particular circumstances. The size and complexity of the organisation will also be a factor in deciding how the agenda should be framed.

- ☐ Apologies for absence.
- ☐ Minutes of previous meeting.
- ☐ Matters arising from those minutes. Some of the matters discussed at the previous meeting may have required additional information before a decision could be made. However, if there are significant points still to be considered it would be preferable for the subject to be dealt with separately as a new item listed in the agenda rather than be dealt with as a matter arising.
- ☐ Other agenda items which may include the following:
  - Receiving and considering the minutes of other committees and sub-committees and matters arising therefrom, particularly items where formal ratification is required.
  - Consideration of periodic reports.
  - In the case of a larger charity receiving and considering progress and other reports from heads of department and senior management.
  - Consideration of specific matters, for example the acquisition of a new property or an extension to an existing one.
  - The appointment of new staff or the recruitment of volunteers.
  - Any other business. It is usual to include this item to give members an opportunity to raise a matter not on the agenda. It may be something which is relatively minor or possibly may be a more urgent matter in which case a decision or action may be required. If, however, a matter which is raised under this heading is of substance and requires further investigation, or if it is thought politic that the views of other members who are not present should be sought, it should be held over until the next meeting.
  - The final item should of course be the fixing or confirmation of the date and venue of the next meeting.

Accompanying papers

The way in which a meeting operates and its effectiveness depends on the information made available to it in good time beforehand. A meeting can become protracted if members have to be informed or reminded of the background to each matter being discussed. Brief details of each item of business should therefore be set out in the agenda itself or in an accompanying document with an identifying reference number. It will then be necessary only for the chairman to bring members up to date with any information received since the agenda was circulated.

Briefing notes

Briefing notes are appropriate for those subjects which do not need a great deal by way of introduction or explanation. Examples include matters dealt with by others which require comment or approval, reports by officials and advisers which need the meeting's decision, straightforward requests for approval of expenditure, and the appointment of staff and recruitment of volunteers.

A briefing note should explain concisely the background to the subject and the action which is required. The notes will be invaluable to the secretary when drafting the minutes of the meeting. If succinct enough briefing notes can be inserted below each item on the agenda or if longer can be issued as a separate document with the notice of the meeting. Neither method is mutually exclusive and a combination can be used where appropriate.

Agenda papers

Accompanying documents are suitable for subjects which either require a great deal of explanation or incorporate a number of factors to be considered. They should be sent with the agenda in order to give members time to consider the issues involved so that they can discuss them with other members prior to the meeting. If practicable the secretary should discuss the agenda before the meeting with the chairman as this often helps to facilitate a better understanding between the trustees and the staff of the charity.

Agenda papers should be numbered serially, with each committee (if more than one) being given its own distinguishing reference. It is advisable to specify the date of the meeting at which the paper is to be considered, particularly if it has been circulated independently of the agenda itself. The originator's name should also appear on the paper. If the nature of the topic warrants it, the secretary should prepare a covering note summarising the background to the matter and those aspects which the meeting is required to decide.

The secretary's role at the meeting

At the meeting the secretary will among other things be responsible for:

- ☐ Notifying apologies for absence.
- ☐ Checking the meeting is properly convened and constituted and that a quorum is present.
- ☐ When necessary amplifying or correcting information already given.
- ☐ Circulating any additional information received since the agenda was issued.
- ☐ Confirming with the chairman the result of any discussion so that the minutes can be accurately drafted.

☐ Drawing the attention of the chairman to any matters which the meeting should consider where it appears these have been overlooked.

Preparation and drafting of minutes

The bane or the delight, as the case may be, of the life of the secretary is the preparation of the minutes. As a general rule minutes should be drafted immediately following the meeting to which they refer. If there is a delay the drafting will become more difficult and time-consuming and if the minutes are not issued promptly there will also be a delay in implementing the decisions reached at the meeting.

What is most important is that each decision taken should be recorded accurately and concisely and where appropriate a note included of who is to take any necessary action. It may also be useful to incorporate a background summary. Any significant points which may have been made in the course of discussion and which show why a particular decision was reached may be included, but not a 'blow-by-blow' account of the proceedings.

7.4 Additional requirements applicable to a charitable company

Articles of association

The articles of association of a charitable company are based on versions prescribed by companies legislation although they have also evolved and developed over many years. In contrast, the governing documents of unincorporated charities are nothing like as uniform and there is an infinite variety; it is this difference which represents the most significant distinction between the governing documents of the two types of organisation.

Meetings of the director/trustees

A charitable company's articles of association usually give the director/trustees the power to regulate their proceedings as they think fit – see clause 51 of Appendix 2. Nonetheless it would be sensible for director/trustees to define the way in which their meetings should be conducted – see for example section 5.2. The articles generally permit the director/trustees to decide how many of their number should constitute a quorum and in the absence of any decision the articles may prescribe what that requirement is to be. As already mentioned, the articles should state whether or not the chairman is to have a second or casting vote. The chairman of a meeting does not have a casting vote unless the articles provide.

The governing documents of many unincorporated charities do not always provide for the chairman of a meeting to have a second or casting vote although the articles of a charitable company usually do.

Frequency of meetings of director/trustees

The meetings of directors of private trading companies are in some cases intermittent and can be informal – although not always. However it is advisable for the meetings of director/trustees of a charitable company to be held regularly, even if infrequently, and for all decisions to be formally minuted which is not only a legal requirement but also good practice; it may also help to avoid the possibility of a breach of trust occurring.

The articles do not usually prescribe the period of notice to be given prior to a meeting of director/trustees, but it would be advisable to agree what this should be, perhaps by passing a resolution to that effect. Alternatively, the dates of board meetings should be fixed for, say, the ensuing year. The articles of association of a charitable company usually provide that a resolution signed by all director/trustees will be as effective as if it had been passed formally at a properly convened meeting. There are rarely similar provisions in the governing document of a charitable unincorporated association or a trust, although such a provision is included in clause 35 of the model constitution in Appendix 1.

Generally speaking it would be advisable for director/trustees not to take advantage of the written resolution procedure but to hold proper meetings as a matter of policy.

7.5 Meetings of the members of a charitable company

Annual general meetings

The way in which meetings of members of a charitable company are to be convened will be prescribed in the articles of association and by the Companies Acts 1985–89. The Companies Act 1985 requires every company to hold an annual general meeting, except where it has passed an elective resolution to dispense with the requirement to hold such a meeting.

The formal ordinary business of an annual general meeting is:

- ☐ To consider the annual report of the director/trustees and the statutory accounts.
- ☐ To consider the report of the auditors.
- ☐ To elect (or re-elect) the director/trustees.
- ☐ To appoint the auditors and fix their remuneration.

Even where the company's auditors are to continue there must still be a formal resolution endorsing their re-appointment unless an elective resolution to dispense with this has previously been passed.

Extraordinary general meetings

Any meeting of the members of a charitable company other than the annual general meeting is an extraordinary general meeting. It is open to the director/trustees to call an extraordinary general meeting, but the 1985 Act also gives the power to 10 per cent of the membership to requisition an extraordinary general meeting. There is no similar provision in trust law generally enabling members of an unincorporated charity to requisition an extraordinary general meeting. It can only be done if the governing document provides – see clause 11 of Appendix 1.

Elective resolutions

Although any private limited company can pass certain elective resolutions one of which is to dispense with the holding of an annual general meeting, it is not advisable for a charitable company to do so because to deny the members the opportunity to meet annually would be counterproductive and could discourage their involvement generally in the activities of the charity.

7.6 Offences for which penalties are prescribed by companies legislation

The relevant section of the Companies Act 1985 as amended by the Companies Act 1989 is stated in the margin.

Meetings of director/trustees

382(5)　The failure to keep minutes of proceedings at board meetings.
450　　 Destroying or mutilating company documents; falsifying documents or making a false entry; parting with documents or altering them or making omissions.
722(3)　The failure to keep minute books securely.

General meetings of members

366(4)　Default in holding an annual general meeting.
367(3)　Default in complying with the Secretary of State's direction to hold a meeting of members.

367(5)   The failure to register a resolution that a meeting held under this section is to be the annual general meeting.
372(4)   The failure to give notice to a member entitled to vote at a company meeting that he may do so by proxy (if the articles so permit).
372(6)   Officer authorising or permitting issue of irregular invitations to appoint proxies (if the articles so permit).
376(7)   Officer failing to circulate members' resolutions.
380(5)   The failure to send copies of certain resolutions to the Registrar.
380(6)   The failure to include a copy of a resolution (to which this section applies) with every copy of the articles subsequently issued, or to forward a copy of any such resolution to a member on request.
382(5)   Default in complying with the requirement to keep minutes of all proceedings of general meetings and meetings of directors.
383(4)   The refusal to allow the inspection of minutes of general meetings; failure to send copies of minutes to a member on request.

7.7   Other useful publications

Shackleton, F. *Law and Practice of Meetings* (1991) Sweet & Maxwell, 8th edition.
The Charities Manual, ICSA Publishing.

8

PROPERTY AND INSURANCE

8.1 Acquisition of freehold or leasehold property

Factors to consider

Most charities do not own property and probably have no involvement with it at all other than as occupiers of premises under the terms of either a lease or a simple licence. For those charities which do own property or are a tenant the following will be relevant. There are a number of factors to consider before acquiring property, for example the location, type of building, any restrictions on use, the nature of any planning permission, whether the property needs adaptation and not least its state of repair.

Even if the governing document does not include a specific power to acquire land there is an implicit assumption that a charity can do so. No order from the Commission is required to authorise an acquisition unless the money being used represents permanent endowment, in which case the Commission may need to authorise the expenditure. The Charity Commission publishes an explanatory leaflet CC38, Expenditure and Replacement of Permanent Endowment.

The Charities Act 1993 gives the Commission the power to authorise certain actions which charity trustees would not otherwise be able to implement and the purchase of land in certain circumstances may fall into this category. To obtain the requisite order a charity would need to instruct a surveyor to inspect the property and to submit a report which must include a description of the property, details of any planning permission required, and a valuation of the property. The Charity Commission leaflet on this topic is CC33, Acquiring Land.

Permitted use

The first question to be asked is, does the intended use of the property comply with any restrictive provisions in the lease, or would there be a breach of any restrictive covenants which affect the freehold title? Some leases have provisions which are very specific as to use and which may be coupled with an absolute prohibition against variation. A charity may be able to negotiate a change of use with the landlord, although some expense may be involved. On the other hand some leases do include a provision that the tenant can apply to the landlord for consent for a change of use, such consent not to be unreasonably withheld.

Freehold properties can be subject to a covenant which restrains the occupier from using the property for a particular purpose, and legal advice should be obtained to see what, if anything, can be done to remove or mitigate the effect of such a restriction.

Planning permission

It is very important to check the planning permission. Although the permission itself may be suitable, the property may have to be adapted. Building regulation consent may therefore be required before any alteration or adaptation can be carried out.

Obtaining the requisite planning permission can sometimes be difficult, especially if the planning authority is, for example, in the process of preparing a local plan and does not want to permit anything which may compromise its review. An application for planning permission can be made by the charity prior to the acquisition of the property provided the requisite statutory notices are served on the existing owner.

Survey

A survey of a property to be acquired should always be carried out. This advice applies generally and not just to an old building or one in a poor state of repair. It may be necessary to adapt a property in which case the estimated cost of carrying out the work should be ascertained before the property is acquired. A surveyor can assist in preparing an estimate and producing a report. Information can then be submitted to the landlord of a leasehold property coupled with a request for consent to the proposed improvements and alterations before the contract for the assignment of the lease is entered into or a new lease is granted.

No such consent will be required in the case of a freehold property but as already stated, building regulation consent may be necessary. It is also important to check the condition of a leasehold property, because a tenant usually has to maintain the building or at least contribute rateably with any other tenants towards its maintenance. The repairing obligation can extend to the building as a whole or to specified parts. This all needs very careful checking.

Purchase of freehold interest

The charity's solicitor, in dealing with the legal aspects of the acquisition of the freehold will check the adequacy of the planning permission, the ownership and responsibility for the maintenance of the boundaries and also obtain replies to various questions which relate to the property generally.

Leases

It is usually more cost-effective for a charity to acquire a lease of premises rather than to fund the purchase of the freehold. What must be appreciated however is that if the charity is the original tenant under a lease entered into before 1 January 1996 (or is indeed an assignee) and a subsequent assignee fails to pay the rent or is in breach of any of the covenants in the lease, the landlord is entitled to claim from the charity (and possibly its trustees) any arrears of rent (together with increases that may have occurred following a rent review) and the cost of putting right any breach of covenant. This is considered in more detail in section 3.4.

Rent review
It is very important that the rent review provisions in the lease are checked thoroughly, as their wording will have a considerable bearing on the outcome of any future rent review negotiations. The implications must be clearly spelt out by the charity's solicitor.

Repairing covenants
The repairing covenant to be observed by the tenant charity should also be fully considered so as to be clear as to what extent and on what basis the charity is liable to contribute to the cost of repairs. As a general rule it is preferable if the landlord retains responsibility for the maintenance of the structure of the building, with the right to recover such expenditure proportionately from each of the tenants by way of an annual service or maintenance charge. It is also important to check how these charges are assessed and how they can be verified by the charity. Another problem with a lease is that if the charity vacates at the end of the lease term, the landlord can usually charge the charity the cost of making good any dilapidations to the premises.

Assignment of the lease
An assignment is normally subject to the landlord's consent not being unreasonably withheld. However, some leases include an absolute prohibition against assignment, and a charity would be advised not to proceed but to look elsewhere, unless of course it is possible to negotiate with the landlord for the removal of such a restriction without undue cost.

Security of tenure

The Landlord and Tenant Act 1954 as amended by the Law of Property Act 1969 gives tenants of business leases some degree of security of tenure. The legislation fortunately applies to property occupied by a charity for the purpose of its objects, although it is possible to exclude the security granted by the legislation if a court order to that effect is insisted upon by the landlord before the lease is granted.

In essence the protection afforded by the legislation means that if at the end of the term specified in the lease, the landlord refuses to grant another lease on a similar basis to the existing one, the charity has the right to apply to the court for an extension of the lease. The court is obliged to grant an extension for a period of up to fourteen years unless the charity has, for example, persistently failed to pay the rent or has been in breach of some other terms of the lease.

There are circumstances in which a landlord can obtain vacant possession notwithstanding the protection given by the 1954 Act, for example if the site is to be redeveloped – but this is comparatively rare.

Licences

Instead of acquiring a leasehold property with all the complications that entails, a charity may consider occupying premises on the basis of a licence or a simple tenancy at will. The advantage is that the charity does not have to comply with the multitude of terms a lease normally contains, nor would it be in the position of having to continue to pay the rent if it no longer required the premises for its own use and was unable to find another occupant.

8.2 Funding an acquisition

Mortgaging charity property

Charities can obtain mortgage funds from a number of sources including banks and building societies. The 1993 Act permits charities to mortgage property which they own or wish to purchase. If the trustees wish to purchase property on mortgage then they must be careful to ensure that the income from the land being acquired is sufficient, after deduction of the cost of any outgoings, to be able to meet the mortgage repayments and to provide an adequate return on any sum invested. Trustees do not require the consent of the Commission to create a mortgage over charity land provided the governing document permits and they have dealt with the matters contained in s. 38 of the 1993 Act and have taken appropriate advice. These matters are:

- [ ] Whether the proposed loan is necessary in order for the charity trustees to be able to pursue the particular course of action in connection with which the loan is sought by them.
- [ ] Whether the terms of the proposed loan are reasonable having regard to the status of the charity as a prospective borrower.
- [ ] Whether the charity has the ability to repay on those terms the amount proposed to be borrowed.

Status of adviser

For the purposes of s. 38 the advice to be sought by the trustees is the advice of a person who is reasonably believed by the trustees to be qualified by his ability in and practical experience of financial matters; and who has no financial interest in the making of the loan.

8.3 Rating of premises owned or occupied by charities

Charities are entitled to apply to their local rating authority to be excused payment of business rates. Properties owned or occupied by charities are entitled to 80 per cent mandatory rate relief. It is also possible to obtain exemption in respect of the other 20 per cent if a request is made to the local authority to exercise its discretion to do so in favour of the charity.

A charity shop is entitled to business rate relief under the provisions of the Rating (Charities Shops Acts) 1976 provided the shop is used wholly or mainly for the sale of goods donated to the charity and the proceeds of their sale are applied to charitable purposes. There can be a problem if a significant proportion of goods being sold have been bought in by the charity for resale.

8.4 Dispositions of charity land and property

The new regime

A new regime was introduced by the Charities Act 1992 and re-enacted by the Charities Act 1993. The new rules govern the sale of a freehold property owned by a charity or the granting of a lease of charity property for more than seven years and are as follows:

- [ ] Trustees must obtain and consider a written report on the proposed disposition from a qualified surveyor instructed by the trustees and acting exclusively for the charity.

- ☐ Trustees must advertise the proposed disposition for such period and in such manner as the surveyor advises in his report, unless he advises that it would not be in the best interests of the charity to advertise.
- ☐ Trustees must decide having considered the surveyor's report that they are satisfied that the terms on which the disposition is proposed to be made are the best that they can reasonably obtain.
- ☐ The surveyor must be a chartered surveyor or a member of the Incorporated Society of Valuers and Auctioneers.

If charity trustees are proposing to grant a lease for a term of between two and seven years they are required only to obtain advice from someone who they reasonably believe has the requisite ability and practical experience to provide them with competent advice on the proposed letting.

The effect of the new provisions is that charity trustees no longer, except in a few cases, have to apply to the Commission for an order consenting to the sale of the property or the granting of a lease of charity property. If the lease to be granted is for a period of less than two years no advice is required at all – the charity can simply go ahead and let the property but before *any* lease is entered into it may be prudent to obtain from the court an order under the Landlord and Tenant Act 1954 excluding the right of the tenant to renew at the end of the term. The charity's solicitor would deal with such an application.

Position of trustees

It is important to note the legal position of charity trustees in relation to transactions involving the charity's assets. They are personally liable for any loss of charity money which results from their dealing with any of its assets in a manner not authorised by the governing document or not in accordance with general trust law.

8.5 Buildings and contents insurance

Duty to insure

Charity trustees are required so far as is reasonable to insure all the charity's property to its full value against risks of physical loss or damage including fire or theft. They are also required to obtain insurance in respect of public liability and, if appropriate, employers' liability. Usually a single policy can be obtained which provides all or most aspects of the required insurance cover. The trustees and the secretary should remember that in making an application for insurance cover there must be full disclosure of all the facts material to the risks which are to be assumed by the insurance company.

Any non-disclosure may invalidate the insurance and if that happens the trustees and the secretary could be liable personally to make good any loss or damage.

Insurance against damage to buildings by fire and other risks

In many cases the premises occupied by the charity and any other property it owns will probably represent its largest capital investment. The necessary fire insurance cover must therefore be carefully managed. Advice should be obtained from an insurance broker or the charity's own surveyor, and a regular review of the extent of the cover carried out. There are two types of insurance cover, one on an indemnity basis and the other on a reinstatement basis.

If the insurance is on an indemnity basis the insurer agrees to pay to the insured the actual loss sustained or to pay for the necessary repairs. Reinstatement cover is different in that the insurer will meet the cost of reinstating what has been destroyed to its pre-existing condition so far as practicable. Cover should be on the basis of the current rebuilding cost of the premises plus an allowance for the cost of demolition, site clearance and surveyors' and other professional fees.

Contents insurance

The contents of any office or building owned or occupied by the charity should be separately insured against loss or damage arising from the usual risks. The extent to which items of office equipment on hire or lease should be insured is debatable, but generally anything of value at the premises ought to be covered. An extension to the policy may be required if high value items are periodically removed temporarily to another location.

8.6 Other insurances

Employers' liability insurance

The occupier of business premises has a statutory duty to ensure so far as is reasonably practicable the health, safety and welfare of all employees while they are at work. It is compulsory for an employer to take out the necessary insurance to meet potential claims by employees who suffer injury at work. The level of cover must be unlimited. The premium payable will usually be assessed by reference to the number of employees and the level of the annual wage and salary costs. A certificate confirming that such a policy is currently in force must be displayed at each workplace.

Public liability insurance

If premises are open to visitors the occupier has a duty to make sure that they are reasonably safe. Appropriate insurance cover must also be arranged. The sum insured should be assessed by reference to the number of employees in the organisation and how many visitors might reasonably be expected to be on the premises at any one time. In the case of one leading charity the cover of £5 million is calculated on the basis of 400 direct and contracted employees and almost the same number of residents living in sheltered accommodation.

Specific insurance cover

Particular charities may require all or any of the following cover:

- ☐ engineering plant and equipment
- ☐ fund-raising events and/or exhibitions
- ☐ vehicles
- ☐ computer equipment and software
- ☐ the cost of re-housing beneficiaries, for example if a residential home was damaged or destroyed
- ☐ trustee liability

8.7 Insurance checklist

The following is a summary of what should be done to manage a charity's insurance risks and cover:

- ☐ A trustee, employee or adviser should be given the responsibility for identifying and monitoring the various risks, and regular reports should be submitted to the trustees. Insurance could be a regular agenda item to be discussed at trustee meetings.
- ☐ A trustee, employee or adviser should be nominated to negotiate the rates of premium prior to the annual renewal of cover and sufficient time should be allowed for any negotiations.
- ☐ An adequate record-keeping system should be installed and reviewed from time to time for accuracy to ensure that details of policies, the extent of the cover and the policy expiry date(s) are properly monitored.
- ☐ A system should be agreed and implemented so that any incident which is likely to lead to a claim is reported to management as soon as is practicable to allow sufficient time for investigation and to prevent a re-occurrence.
- ☐ Responsibility for notifying any incidents and claims either to the brokers or the insurers should be given to a nominated individual, usually the secretary.

☐ A valuer or surveyor should be appointed to provide valuations for insurance purposes annually.

This checklist is not exhaustive and the requirements will vary from one charity to another.

8.8 Other useful publications

Carter, R.G. *Handbook of Insurance*, Kluwer Publications.
Martin, D. *One Stop Property*, ICSA Publishing.

The Charity Commission publishes:

CC3   Responsibilities of Charity Trustees
CC28 Disposing of Charity Land
CC33 Acquiring Land
CC38 Expenditure and Replacement of Permanent Endowment
CC49 Charities and Insurance

NCVO publishes:

Insurance Protection: A Guide for Voluntary Organisations
Trustee Liability Insurance

9

FUND-RAISING

9.1 Background

Legislation

Fund-raising is the lifeblood of most charities. However, it is beyond the scope of this book to deal with the subject other than in outline, although The Charitable Institutions (Fund-Raising) Regulations 1994 and the essentials of a fund-raising agreement between a charity and a fund-raiser are included.

Sources

Fund-raising can take a number of different forms and varies from the straightforward collection of money in boxes or envelopes to a fully researched and comprehensive programme to raise a substantial amount for capital investment. Fund-raising by most charities is usually limited to one or two tried and tested methods. Few have the resources to undertake anything more ambitious. In contrast, some of the larger charities have their own fund-raising department which is usually very professional and businesslike.

The main sources of funds are donations, collections, legacies, covenants, retail trading and grants, although payroll and Gift Aid are other important sources. Last but not least there is the National Lottery.

9.2 Legacies

Potential

Legacies generally represent a more important source of income for large charities, the RNLI being a good example. However, this does not mean that smaller charities do not receive legacies. Some local charities, for example, receive substantial amounts from the estates of individuals.

Types of bequest

The gift in a will of a specific asset, perhaps property or some other valuable item, is known as a specific bequest. A gift of a specified amount of money is known as a pecuniary legacy. A bequest which entitles the charity to the balance of what is left after all other bequests have been made and debts paid is known as a residuary legacy or bequest.

Any gift or legacy to a charity under a will is exempt from inheritance tax, a useful point to emphasise when seeking legacies.

Model form of wording to be incorporated into wills and codicils

A charity should consider having its own particular form of wording for use when someone making a will proposes to include the charity as a beneficiary. Solicitors who are preparing a will which is to include a bequest to a charity may ask the charity to provide its form of preferred wording and it is therefore advisable to have a draft precedent available. A number of larger charities publish helpful leaflets or booklets giving advice on the making of wills which often include precedent clauses.

Contacting existing supporters

This is something that comes more easily to some than others, but contacting the supporters of a charity should be considered suggesting that when the supporter is making a will the charity should be included as a beneficiary. One method of encouraging this would be to include an appropriate item in a newsletter.

9.3   Covenants

Tax efficiency

Although in recent years there has been a move away from covenants in the wake of Gift Aid and payroll giving, nonetheless a covenant is a very effective way for a charity to raise funds. This is especially true of small to medium-sized charities which may not have the resources or capacity to become too involved in Gift Aid and other forms of direct giving which can be complicated to administer and also time-consuming to set up.

A charity is able to reclaim the tax from the Inland Revenue which a donor has already borne at the basic rate on the same amount of his income as the sum specified in the covenant. In addition a higher rate taxpayer can claim personally the difference between the basic rate and the higher rate of tax which he has paid to the Revenue in respect of the sums to be contributed under a deed of covenant.

The other advantage from the charity's point of view is that a covenant represents a more reliable source of income. A covenant must be expressed to continue for a period exceeding three years. A word of caution though in the light of a 1995 case: the payment dates must be spread over a period greater than three years and it should be clear that the payments do not (or cannot) fall due within a shorter period. It is therefore advisable that a covenant should be expressed to continue for four years. The donor/covenantor has the option to cancel the covenant within the specified period if he wishes to do so, and the charity agrees, without affecting the validity of the covenant for the period it actually continues to be in force.

An advantage from a charity's point of view is that the donor is able to give a greater amount as the payments are spread over a period of time. On the other hand some donors do not want to be committed for such a long time, although a covenant can subsequently be cancelled with the consent of the charity. Donors can also be reluctant to complete the necessary paperwork, which can be time-consuming. The resistance may be partly overcome by offering to help the donor to complete the forms and witness his signature.

What is a covenant?

A covenant is a legal document but is not itself a tax form. To be effective it has to comply with various legal requirements. A precedent covenant form appears on page 114. This form is suitable for use by most charities. It also gives the donor the option to pay by instalments throughout the year and suitably adapted it can be used, for example, by schools. The disadvantage is that as the payments are more frequent the more the donor is likely to pay by way of bank charges.

It is important to remember that the deed of covenant is what it says – a deed – and therefore has to be executed as such. This means that the signature of the donor has to be witnessed. It is also important that the date the covenant is signed is correct and that the first payment does not become due prior to the date on which the covenant itself is signed.

9.4 Lotteries

The legislation

Lotteries, or as they are often described, raffles or tombolas, can take place only as permitted by the Lotteries & Amusements Act 1976, as amended by the National Lottery Act 1993.

Kinds of lottery

There are three kinds of lottery relevant to charities: small lotteries incidental to certain types of entertainment, private lotteries and society lotteries.

A small lottery
This is usually held at a social event or fete. The whole of the proceeds of any entertainment which is provided together with the proceeds of the lottery must be paid to the charity after any deductions. No money can be given as a prize and ticket sales must take place during the social event. The lottery has to be incidental to the main purpose of the social event and the result must be announced at the time. The maximum that can be spent on providing prizes is £250. A small lottery does not need to be registered.

A private lottery
Tickets can be sold only to members of the charity or other persons who are closely associated with it. After deduction of expenses the balance of the net proceeds must be utilised to provide prizes. Any advertising is limited to the premises of the charity, and there are various other fairly restrictive conditions. However, a private lottery, for example, a tombola or raffle at a major fund-raising function such as a gala ball can be an important part of 'event' fund-raising.

A society lottery
This is the type of lottery which is most likely to be of use to a charity. The charity would first have to register with the Gaming Board of Great Britain if the value of the tickets on sale exceeds £20,000. If less, the charity should register with the local authority. The advantage of this kind of lottery is that tickets can be sold to the general public; although the value of prizes must not be more than half of the total proceeds these can be either cash or in kind. The name of the promoter who must be connected with the charity has to appear on every ticket. A fee is payable on registration and an annual payment is required to renew the registration. Any secretary thinking of organising such a lottery should obtain the explanatory leaflets mentioned in section 9.10.

9.5   Charity trading companies

Eligibility

Charities are entitled to trade in order to attain the purpose for which they are established. For example, a charity whose purpose is the advancement of education can charge fees, and a charity established for purposes beneficial to the community can charge for the services it provides even if only nominally. A number of private hospitals are charities and charge accordingly.

Trading which is ancillary to the main objects of the charity

There are a variety of ancillary activities, for example operating a cafe for use by visitors to a museum, selling goods received from donors, and running a shop at a school for the benefit of students. There is no need to set up a trading company to carry out these types of activity.

A trading company or not?

Where the trading activity does not constitute the primary purpose of the charity but is a separate 'business' in its own right, a trading company may be required. For example the sale of Christmas cards may constitute a significant source of income, in which case it should be conducted through a separate company. However, it is a matter of degree and as already mentioned if the trading activity is ancillary to the main purpose of the charity it may not be necessary to form a separate company. On the other hand, if the sale of Christmas cards is sufficient to constitute a separate and distinct trading activity it should be channelled through a charity trading company.

The same principle applies to a charity which promotes a catalogue sales business. Another popular form of trading which has developed in recent years is for a charity to give permission to a third party commercial participator to use its name. In addition to the requirement for a written agreement in order to comply with the 1994 Regulations, any income derived from this kind of source would be regarded as trading income.

In order to avoid inadvertently creating a tax liability it is advisable for major fund-raising events to be administered through a company but as with much else, professional advice should be sought beforehand.

Establishing a trading company

Normally a trading company would be a limited company with a share capital, unlike a charitable company which is limited by guarantee. Capital can be injected into the company through the issue of shares to the charity, although the issued share capital would not necessarily bear any relation to the value of the company or the level of its trading activity. The charity could instead, subject to certain safeguards, provide capital in the form of a secured loan repayable on notice. Such a loan would though have to carry an appropriate rate of interest.

Considerations to be made before investment

The trustees should carry out some market research to ensure that the business to be transacted through the trading company is financially viable.

They should also prepare initial budgets and cashflow forecasts, together with a business plan. The trading company must be run on a sound business footing, and if it is not and loss results the trustees of the charity and also the directors of the trading company could be made personally liable.

It is also important to devise the form the investment in a trading company should take and whether any money so invested should be subject to the payment of interest at a commercial rate. The Commission has issued its own guidelines in this respect, one of which requires that interest should be paid to the charity – see leaflet CC35. The guidelines also require that security for any loan be given by the trading company to the charity, possibly by way of a debenture. There are a number of factors to be considered and the setting up of a trading company is not something to be undertaken lightly. At all stages in the process professional advice should be sought.

In particular, a profit-shedding deed of covenant should be professionally prepared to ensure that any profits are received by the charity itself as annual payments. If this is not done, any payment made to the charity by the trading company will be regarded as a distribution on which corporation tax will be payable.

9.6 Capital fund-raising

Purpose

Some charities require the input of a large amount of money for a particular capital project, for example the refurbishment of a theatre, cathedral, or other building.

The appeal plan

The plan should be as detailed and comprehensive as possible showing clearly the way in which the appeal will be conducted. An appeal budget should be prepared and agreed by the trustees either in conjunction with the charity's own fund-raising staff or a fund-raising consultant or professional fund-raiser if any. Expenditure can be considerable and will include the cost of any literature, brochures, acquisition of office equipment, stationery and postage and if the appeal is to raise money for a new building or similar, the expense of preparing the necessary plans and obtaining planning consent.

9.7 Use of consultants and professional fund-raisers

Written agreement

There are a number of professional fund-raisers who can assist with a capital fund-raising venture or a revenue-raising project or programme. It is important that any agreement between a charity and a fund-raising consultant or professional fund-raiser should be in writing. Any such written agreement should be vetted by the charity's own solicitor to make sure that the position of the charity is properly protected and also that the agreement complies with the provisions of the Charitable Institutions (Fund-Raising) Regulations 1994.

Fund-raising consultant

A consultant is someone who provides fund-raising advisory services to a charity but does not solicit directly or indirectly for donations or other property on behalf of the charity. A consultant will, depending on the extent of the services to be provided, be involved in composing advertising material and requests for donations and will usually also help to devise the fund-raising strategy and suggest which donors or range of donors should be approached for support. In order to preserve his status as a consultant (and so as not to become a professional fund-raiser) the consultant must ensure that there is no direct or indirect contact by him with donors or potential donors. Technically no written agreement is necessary, but nonetheless it would be prudent for the charity to enter into an agreement so that its interests are protected and each party knows what the other is to do and how any payments due to the consultant are to be assessed and made.

Professional fund-raiser

A professional fund-raiser is either an individual or a company which both advises and acts on behalf of a charitable institution in order to raise funds. A fund-raiser will not only advise the charity with regard to the strategy and targeting of potential sources of funds but is also very likely to solicit for funds on behalf of the charity and also collect those funds before passing them on to the charity. The very fact that the fund-raiser solicits funds on behalf of the charity means that a written agreement as required by the Charities Act 1992 and the 1994 Regulations is a pre-requisite. In addition a professional fund-raiser may be responsible for the preparation of brochures and advertising material although the cost of doing so will usually be borne by the charity.

Questions to ask a consultant or a professional fund-raiser

It will usually fall to the charity secretary to conduct any negotiations with a consultant or a professional fund-raiser and it would be as well to think about the questions it would be prudent to ask before any written agreement is entered into. The following are examples of the kinds of matters to raise:

- ☐ On what basis would any charges be made: daily, weekly or monthly and how frequently would invoices be submitted and how detailed would these be?
- ☐ What level of travel expenses are likely to be incurred, and how would such expenses be assessed and how would they be reimbursed?
- ☐ What target is feasible and how would the scale of giving by donors be structured?
- ☐ What form of agreement is it proposed the consultant or fund-raiser should offer and is a draft available for consideration?
- ☐ What are the proposals regarding any prior determination of the agreement and how would any outstanding obligations be dealt with?
- ☐ What timescale is involved, and if a resources study is to be prepared how long would it take and what would be the cost?
- ☐ What kind of strategy is likely to be devised and over how long a period could it be implemented?
- ☐ Can the consultant or fund-raiser provide any professional and financial references?
- ☐ What level of responsibility does the consultant or fund-raiser accept so far as compliance with various legal requirements is concerned?
- ☐ What kind of 'track record' does the consultant or fund-raiser have?

Commercial participator

A commercial participator is anyone who is in business for gain, which although not a fund-raising business, carries out in the course of such business a sales campaign or conducts other promotional activity stating that contributions will be made to a charity or charitable cause. Consequently a written agreement in the prescribed form must be made between the charity and the commercial participator and any such agreement should take into account the provisions to be included in a fund-raising agreement.

9.8 Checklist of provisions to be included in a fund-raising agreement

Requirements of the 1994 Regulations

The Regulations set out certain provisions which have to be included in a written agreement between a charity and a professional fund-raiser (not a consultant who acts strictly in that capacity) but there are a number of other matters – see below – which should be included in such an agreement so that the charity's position is properly protected.

The Regulations prescribe that the agreement shall be in writing and be signed by or on behalf of the charitable institution and the professional fund-raiser and that the following matters should be specified or contained in such agreement:

- [ ] The name and address of each of the parties to the agreement.
- [ ] The date on which the agreement was signed by or on behalf of each of those parties.
- [ ] The period for which the agreement is to subsist.
- [ ] Any terms relating to the termination of the agreement prior to the date on which that period expires.
- [ ] Any terms relating to the variation of the agreement during that period.
- [ ] A statement of the principal objectives and the methods to be used in pursuit of those objectives.
- [ ] If there is more than one charitable institution which is a party to the agreement the way in which the benefits accruing to each institution is to be determined.
- [ ] Provision as to the amount by way of remuneration or expenses which the professional fund-raiser is to be entitled to receive in respect of things done by him in pursuance of the agreement and the manner in which that amount is to be determined.

Additional matters which should be included in a written agreement with a professional fund-raiser

The Regulations specify only those requirements listed above but ideally the following matters should also be included in order to protect the charity's interests and to make it certain how the charity and the fund-raiser are to discharge their respective obligations.

- [ ] A statement setting out *precisely* the nature and extent of the advice and services to be provided by the fund-raiser.
- [ ] Details of the commitment in terms of the number of person hours to be provided by the fund-raiser.
- [ ] The frequency with which VAT invoices are to be submitted and the timescale within which payment of invoices is to be made.
- [ ] A requirement that the fund-raiser maintains confidentiality with regard to all information obtained in respect of the charity.
- [ ] A requirement (if appropriate) that the fund-raiser should install any software which may be necessary for the purposes of the campaign.
- [ ] A statement that the fund-raiser accepts that he is responsible for the accuracy and the form and content of any written material issued in connection with the campaign.
- [ ] A requirement that the fund-raiser obtains any necessary consents from the regulatory authorities.

- ☐ A requirement that the fund-raiser prepares periodic financial statements showing in detail any amounts received, the sources and the period of time involved.
- ☐ An obligation that the fund-raiser should maintain books of account, documents and any other records as required by the legislation.
- ☐ A statement that the agreement is exclusive to the fund-raiser and not capable of assignment.
- ☐ An indemnity by the fund-raiser in respect of any proceedings, claims, costs, etc. that may result from his activities.
- ☐ Provisions setting out how any money or other property acquired by the fund-raiser and due to the charity should be transmitted to the charity and how frequently.

This is not an exhaustive list. A number of matters will need to be taken into account depending on the particular circumstances of each individual campaign and will depend particularly on the purpose for which the money is being raised. There are many potential pitfalls and traps for the unwary and time spent in making sure that the agreement satisfies all the charity's requirements is an investment worth making.

Many of the points discussed in this paragraph should also be borne in mind in reaching any agreement with a fund-raising consultant.

9.9 Precedent form of deed of covenant

See page 114.

9.10 Other useful publications

ICSA Publishing publishes:

Mullin, R. *Foundations for Fund-Raising* (1994).
Bruce, I. *Charity Marketing: Meeting Need* (1997).

NCVO publishes:

Fundraising by Charities
Government Grants
A Guide for Voluntary Organisations
Lotteries and Gaming
Voluntary Organisations and the Media

The Directory of Social Change publishes:

Raising Money for Trusts
A Guide to the Major Grant Making Trusts

Raising Money from Industry
A Guide to Company Giving
Industrial Sponsorship and Joint Promotions
Raising Money from Government
Charity Trading Handbook
Legacies – a Practical Guide for Charities

Other:

Charity Commission CC20: Charities and Fund-raising
Gaming Board Booklet: Lotteries and the Law
Home Office Guidance Notes for Lotteries Registered with Local Authorities
Home Office Guide to Part II Charitable Fund-raising: Professional and Commercial Involvement

PRECEDENT FORM OF COMBINED DEED OF COVENANT AND BANKERS' ORDER FORM

DEED OF COVENANT

I, ...

of ....

.... Postcode ....

undertake to pay (Name of Charity):

*(a) on   November,   February and   April in each year commencing on   November 199

OR

*(b) annually commencing on the   November 199

for the next 4 years, such sums out of my taxed income that will, after deduction of income tax at the basic rate, be £ .... ** for each period/*year

SIGNED as a Deed and delivered by me this .... day of ....199+

Signature: ....

Witness' signature: ....

and address: ....

Your signature should be witnessed by an adult other than a member of your family.

* Delete which is inapplicable
** The figure to be put here is the actual amount that you wish to pay, either on each of the 3 payment dates during the course of each year, or annually, as you prefer.
+ This must be the same as, or earlier than the date of your first payment shown in the bankers' order form below.

BANKERS' ORDER FORM

Bank Name: ....

Bank Address: ....

....

Please pay to the account of (Name of Charity)
(Account No.) at   Bank Plc, (Address) (Sort Code)

*(a) The sum of £ .... on   November 199 and then on   February,   April and November in each year until   April 199

OR

*(b) The sum of £ .... on   November 199 and then each year on   November until   November 199

Name of account to be debited: ....

Bank Account No: ....

Signature(s): ....

Date: .... Mr/Mrs/Ms ....

Address: ....

.... Postcode ....

Telephone No: ....

*Delete which is inapplicable

10

PERSONNEL ADMINISTRATION AND EMPLOYMENT LAW AND PRACTICE

10.1 The contract of employment

The nature of an employment contract

Despite all the employment legislation there has been in recent years the basis of the relationship between employer and employee remains the contract which can be oral, in writing or partly both. A distinction should though be drawn between a contract of employment and an arrangement under which services are provided by an individual in return for payment but which does not amount to employment in the legal sense.

Certain employees particularly those in a senior management role may be able to negotiate their terms of employment in quite some detail but in the normal employer/employee relationship any negotiation of the terms and conditions of employment is limited. Not only that, but in many cases the contract will be oral and not in writing, despite the legal obligation on the part of an employer to provide the written statement of the main terms mentioned later. A problem which can arise in respect of an oral contract is proving what was actually agreed between the employer and employee.

Not all terms have to be specified because a number are implied by the law automatically, and therefore included without specific mention. With all contracts (not only contracts of employment) it is important to distinguish between implied terms and express terms. Express terms are those which are specifically included in the contract or agreement.

A written contract will prove its worth if relations between the parties break down and the employee subsequently brings a claim to an industrial tribunal for compensation alleging unfair dismissal.

Employment terms

A written contract has apart from anything else the effect of removing any doubts about what was agreed between the parties at the outset.

As already mentioned, it is not necessary for a *contract* of employment to be in writing, although as will be seen on page 117 below an employer is legally obliged to provide an employee with a written statement of the main terms and conditions of employment, which although not amounting to a contract as such, does represent the best evidence of what has been agreed between the parties.

Whether an employment contract is written or is oral there are, in addition to the written statement of terms and conditions, various matters which should preferably be agreed between the employer and the employee. To some extent it depends on the scope of the job, but for example could include the following:

- ☐ The name of the person or his title to whom the employee is directly responsible.
- ☐ The basis on which travelling and other out-of-pocket expenses are to be claimed.
- ☐ Confidentiality provisions.
- ☐ How flexible the employee is expected to be to meet the requirements of the employer.
- ☐ Any obligation on the part of the employee to work overtime and the basis on which any payment would be made.
- ☐ A restriction on the employee from working for a competitor employer and the basis and timescale considered reasonable.

The obligations of charities as employers

The first obligation, not surprisingly, is that the employee must be paid for the work done. Secondly, and very important, the charity must operate a safe system of work which means that it has to ensure that all employees (and volunteers for that matter) are not put at risk. One practical example is to ensure that employees do not behave in such a way as to cause physical or other risks to fellow employees and that if there is plant and machinery the charity complies with all statutory requirements regarding its use.

The obligations of employees

The first obligation of an employee is to be available for work. Secondly, the employee must comply with the lawful directions of the employer, but not to the extent that to do so would put the employee at risk to an unacceptable degree or which requires him to behave in such a way that breaks the law. An employee must also take reasonable care because if he is negligent the employer can in principle sue the employee for any damage or loss directly arising from such negligence.

Another very important element of the employer/employee relationship is confidentiality. Employees must not generally disclose confidential information they obtain through their employment although there are limits to this. If an employer wishes to protect confidential information the better option is to include a confidentiality clause in a written contract of employment although it should be remembered that such a clause must be reasonable and not too draconian. This may not be so relevant in the case of a charity but nonetheless should be considered particularly in respect of, for example, any information which relates to donors.

Written statement to be provided by an employer

As already mentioned, an employer has a statutory duty to provide the employee with a written statement of the terms and conditions of employment. This requirement is contained in s.1 of the Employment Rights Act 1996. With a few exceptions all employees including part-time employees must receive the written statement within two months of starting employment. The written statement comprises the following:

- [ ] The names of the employer and employee.
- [ ] The date when the employment began.
- [ ] The date on which the employee's period of continuous employment began.
- [ ] Either the place of work or the location where the employee is required or permitted to work and the address of the employer.
- [ ] The scale or rate of remuneration or the method of calculating the remuneration.
- [ ] The intervals at which the remuneration is to be paid, i.e. weekly, monthly or otherwise.
- [ ] Any terms and conditions relating to hours of work including normal hours.
- [ ] The title of the job which the employee is employed to do or a brief description of the work for which the employee is employed.
- [ ] Entitlement to holidays including public holidays and holiday pay.
- [ ] Where the employment is not intended to be permanent the period for which it is expected to continue or if it is for a fixed term the date when it is to end.
- [ ] Any collective agreements (with trade unions) which directly affect the terms and conditions of the employment including, where the employer

is not a party, a statement of those persons by whom such collective agreements were made.
- ☐ Where the employee is required to work outside the UK for a period of more than one month, details of where and for how long.
- ☐ Whether a contracting out certificate is in force for the employment.
- ☐ Where the employee is unable to work due to sickness or injury, the basis on which the employee will be entitled to sick pay.
- ☐ Details of any pension entitlement and pension schemes.
- ☐ The length of notice which the employee is obliged to give and entitled to receive to terminate the employment.
- ☐ A note specifying any disciplinary rules applicable to the employee or a reference to a document to which the employee has access containing such rules.
- ☐ A note specifying by description or otherwise a person to whom the employee can apply if he is dissatisfied with any disciplinary decision and a person to whom the employee can apply for the purpose of seeking redress of any grievance relating to his employment and the manner in which any such application has to be made.
- ☐ Where there are further steps consequent on any such application a note of what they are.

The written statement given in accordance with s.1 of the Employment Rights Act 1996 cannot be changed except by the employer giving the employee one month's written notice.

Payment of wages and an itemised pay statement

An employer must provide all employees with an itemised pay statement as required by the Employment Rights Act 1996 which must specify the gross pay, the net pay and any deductions from the gross pay showing the amounts deducted and why such deductions have been made. There is, however, no standard form of pay slip and it is therefore not always easy for an employee to work out the way in which his pay has been computed.

Deduction from wages

The Employment Rights Act 1996 precludes an employer from making deductions from an employee's wages. However, there are some exceptions. These include an attachment of earnings order issued by a court to an employer requiring deductions to be made from an employee's wages or if the employment contract itself includes a term stating that certain deductions can be made.

There is also a limit applicable to an employer who carries on a retail business which a number of charities do. Such an employer can only deduct up to one-tenth of the gross amount of an employee's wages and even then deductions can only be made in respect of a deficiency which has occurred within a twelve-month period beforehand. Different rules apply in the case of an employee who is leaving.

Entitlement to sick pay

The extent to which an employee is entitled to sick pay from his employer depends on any provision contained in the contract of employment. The written statement which the employer is obliged to issue must say whether or not sick pay is payable. The majority of employees are entitled to statutory sick pay which is a payment made by the employer and in respect of which the employer can subsequently recover the amount of SSP paid in a tax month which exceeds the specified percentage.

Disciplinary procedures

Although an employee must usually do as the employer requires, there will be occasions when the employee does not or cannot comply. There are certain consequences which follow should that happen.

First, an employer has the option of dismissing the employee. However, in many instances the sacked employee would probably be able to apply to an industrial tribunal claiming unfair dismissal and seeking compensation. If the employee has behaved so badly the employer may not have had any other option but to dismiss the employee without notice immediately, i.e. summarily. Otherwise an employer would be advised to comply with the code of practice issued by ACAS, which specifies the disciplinary rules and procedures which should be followed in such cases. ACAS is an acronym for the Advisory Conciliation and Arbitration Service. The ACAS code specifies among other things the sequence of events which the employer should follow. These are:

- ☐ The employee should be informed of the nature of the complaint which has been made.
- ☐ The employee should be given sufficient opportunity to explain his conduct.
- ☐ The employer must then decide how to proceed. If the behaviour or conduct is not so serious the employer can issue a formal oral warning but if the misconduct is more serious a formal written warning should be considered. A written warning should preferably set out what the consequences will be if the employee's performance does not improve or there is a repetition of the poor behaviour.

If the employee's behaviour is fairly serious an employer can instead of issuing a first oral or written warning issue a final written warning stating that any future breach by the employee will automatically lead to dismissal or suspension. If the behaviour of the employee has been particularly grave or serious the employer can consider instant dismissal but only where the circumstances are sufficient to justify that course of action. Instant dismissal in practice is quite rare.

10.2 Job security

Notice to terminate employment

As already mentioned, the relationship between employer and employee is one of contract. If either party wishes to terminate the contract one party must first give notice to the other.

Notice by the employer

As will have already been noted, there may not necessarily be a written contract of employment, nor may an employer have complied with the statutory obligation to provide a written statement of the terms and conditions of employment within two months of the start date. The length of notice an employer must give to an employee in the absence of anything in writing to the contrary in order to comply with the statutory minimum periods prescribed by the Employment Rights Act 1996 are:

Length of employment	*Length of notice by employer*
Under one month	Nil
One month–two years	One week
Two years–twelve years	One week for each full year of employment
Over twelve years	Twelve weeks

If an employee has worked for between one month and a year but has been paid on a monthly basis and there is nothing in writing to the contrary it could be argued that he is entitled to one month's pay and not just the one week which is the statutory minimum. However, the cost of bringing any court proceedings to enforce such a claim is likely to be prohibitive.

Paying wages in lieu of notice

It is not necessary for an employee to continue working if the employer does not want the employee to do so and is prepared to pay wages in lieu for the notice period.

Circumstances in which it is not necessary for the employer to give any notice

Dismissal without notice may occur where the employee's conduct is sufficient to justify summary dismissal. Examples of such serious misconduct are theft or assault on a fellow employee.

Gross misconduct sufficient to justify immediate dismissal

The behaviour of the employee must be so bad and unacceptable as fundamentally to destroy the contractual relationship. An industrial tribunal, however, would consider summary dismissal to be justified in only exceptional circumstances. Even if on the face of it the dismissal is justified, nonetheless the employee must be given an opportunity to give his own account of what happened. If instant dismissal does not prove to be justified an employee can claim against an employer for:

- ☐ wages due to him for the period of notice on the ground of wrongful dismissal and/or
- ☐ compensation for unfair dismissal because the employer's action in sacking the employee was unreasonable and unjustified.

When proper notice has not been given

Unless the situation can be resolved by negotiation the course of action available to an employee would be simply to sue the employer for breach of contract claiming any salary or wages due in respect of the notice period. As the employer unreasonably broke a term of the contract he would be liable to pay damages, but only after the employee has instigated court action if agreement could not be reached. One of the problems, however, is that the amount of money involved is unlikely to be enough to encourage an employee to go to the time, trouble and expense of issuing court proceedings.

Giving reasons for dismissal

An employer is obliged to give written reasons to an employee following his dismissal but only if the employee has worked for more than two years. It is not however automatic and the onus is on the employee to ask the employer to comply. It would be advisable for an employee to make any such request in writing. The employer's answer must be adequate and give sufficient information and detail.

Notice by the employee

An employee must give one week's notice if he has been employed for more than four weeks. If the contract of employment stipulates a longer period of notice the employee must comply accordingly. Similarly, where a written statement has been issued by the employer the employee must give the period of notice specified in that statement.

If the employee resigns without giving proper notice

In the same way as an employer would be in breach of contract for giving insufficient notice so would an employee. The employer in principle could bring court action against the employee claiming damages. It is not normally worth an employer doing so because the loss incurred is usually not very great and when balanced against the time, effort and expense involved in taking such action the employer will generally come to the conclusion that it is not commercially viable.

References and testimonials

Contrary to popular belief an employer is not obliged to give an employee a reference. This is so notwithstanding the adverse effect it may have on an employee's chances of getting another job. If a reference is provided then it must be truthful even if the truth may not be very welcome. Provided the reference is given honestly and without malice an employer will not be liable if an employee failed to obtain alternative employment.

Redundancy

When an employee is redundant he may be entitled to a redundancy payment. However, if the employee's job still exists but is subsequently filled by someone else the employee may nevertheless be redundant if there has been a net loss of jobs in the organisation or in one of the units of that organisation.

Subject to there being a redundancy situation an employee will qualify for payment if he has worked for an employer for at least two years and for eight hours or more a week. Employment under the age of 18 does not count. The employee will receive between half and one-and-a-half week's pay for each year of employment depending on his age. The limit is currently £210 per week although it is reviewed annually by Parliament. The maximum number of years for which the redundant employee can qualify is twenty years. If an employee unreasonably refuses an offer by the employer of alternative work then he will lose his entitlement to a redundancy payment. However, the offer has to be reasonable. It would not be reasonable to offer a low-paid worker an alternative job which involved, for example, moving house even if alternative accommodation was available.

Any employee who is being made redundant and who has been employed for two years or more is entitled to a reasonable amount of time off with pay to try and arrange training or to obtain another job.

Employing illegal immigrants

The Asylum and Immigration Act 1996 came into force on 27 January 1997. It creates the criminal offence of employing a person who does not have permission to live and work in the UK, although there is a defence available to employers who make certain checks before taking on a new employee. The maximum fine on conviction is £5,000.

The Home Office has published useful guidance for employers which is designed to help understand the new rules. The Commission for Racial Equality was involved in the preparation of the guidance which makes the point that the best way to ensure that employers do not discriminate against job applicants on the ground of race is to treat every applicant in the same way at each stage of the recruitment process. This new law is applicable to charities as it is to any other employer.

10.3 Unfair dismissal

Outline of the system

An employee who considers that he has been unfairly dismissed can make a claim for compensation to an industrial tribunal. The industrial tribunal regime was introduced in 1971. Up until then employees had very little redress if they were dismissed, even though they may have worked for the same employer for many years. The industrial tribunal system was introduced by the Industrial Relations Act 1971, although the current law regarding unfair dismissal is contained in the Employment Rights Act 1996 and the Industrial Tribunals Act 1996.

The right of a dismissed employee to make a claim to an industrial tribunal can be expressed as follows:

Any employee who has worked for an employer for two years or more must within three months of the termination of his employment complain in writing to an industrial tribunal, using the standard form available for this purpose. If the dismissed employee can prove to the tribunal that he has been dismissed then it is up to the employer to justify the dismissal. An employer must also show that he had a fair reason for dismissing the employee, for example the employee was incompetent or dishonest. The tribunal must then consider whether the employer acted reasonably in making the decision to dismiss the employee. The question then to be decided by the tribunal is whether or not the employer adopted a fair procedure before dismissing the employee. In the event the tribunal decides that the dismissal was unfair it may require the employer to re-instate the employee. Alternatively, and this is more often the case, the employer will be ordered to pay compensation to the employee. If the employee's behaviour has contributed to the dismissal the amount of compensation will be reduced by the proportion which the tribunal considers to be appropriate.

Charities are particularly prone to claims by former employees and therefore avoiding situations which can lead to such claims will not only reduce costs but prevent the loss of valuable management time.

These requirements now need to be looked at in more detail and broken down into their separate and distinct parts.

Does the employee qualify under the unfair dismissal legislation?

As already mentioned, an employee must have been employed for a minimum of two years in order to be able to make a claim in the first place.

Part-time employees

Originally, part-time employees, i.e. those working less than sixteen hours per week, could not bring a claim for unfair dismissal unless they had been employed for at least five years. A European Court decision in 1995 overturned this restriction and now any employee who has worked part-time for at least two years is able to bring a claim for unfair dismissal if the circumstances justify.

Statutory retirement age

Anyone who has reached the normal statutory retirement age cannot claim compensation for unfair dismissal. If a female employee aged 63 was dismissed she would not be able to claim compensation even though her contract of employment may state that the normal retirement age in relation to her employment with that particular employer was 65.

Dismissal on the grounds of race, sex or trade union activities

There is no qualifying period for an employee who claims that he has been dismissed as a result of his race, sex, trade union activities or who has been discriminated against because he is married. Such employees therefore do not have to have worked the two-year period before bringing a claim for unfair dismissal.

Dismissal

In most cases there is no argument about whether or not there has been a dismissal. In the event of dismissal the employee will usually be given any relevant documentation, for example a P45, and will receive payment in lieu of notice. Sometimes, however, the facts do not lead so readily to such a conclusion. It is possible that the employer did not spell out to the employee that he had been dismissed. If that is the case a tribunal would have to consider whether the facts amounted to a dismissal. In one case the employer had been away from work ill for some time and was still recuperating. An argument arose between the employer's son and another employee and the employer intervened telling the employee to 'get out of the premises' in no uncertain terms. The employee did so and complained that he had been unfairly dismissed. However, the tribunal felt that the employer's words had been spoken in the heat of the moment and was in part due to her state of health. The employee should therefore not have regarded himself as having been dismissed.

Constructive dismissal

It may happen that an employee is put in such a situation that he has no option but to resign. If that resignation is fully justified the employee is said to have been constructively dismissed, in which case the employee may be able to claim compensation for unfair dismissal. However, the employer's behaviour must have been so bad as to constitute a fundamental breach of the contract of employment.

A good illustration of this point is demonstrated by the following case. The employer refused to allow a shop assistant a day off or part of the day so that she could be at home when her son returned from hospital. The employee took the time off nonetheless and did not return. She then claimed unfair dismissal. The tribunal however decided that even though the employer had not behaved well there were mitigating reasons. The organisation was a very small one and there was no implied term in the employee's contract that she should be able to have time off even in the circumstances of this case. Consequently the tribunal held that the employee had not been constructively dismissed.

This decision may perhaps be thought rather harsh. Initially industrial tribunal decisions tended to favour employers rather than employees when deciding questions of constructive dismissal, although to some extent the pendulum has swung to a more even-handed position during the last twenty years or so. In another case a foreman was instructed that he was to work in future supervised by a less experienced electrician, supposedly as a temporary arrangement. The foreman refused, resigned and claimed constructive dismissal. The tribunal decided that there had been a substantial breach of contract and therefore the employee was constructively dismissed and consequently entitled to compensation for unfair dismissal.

Did the employer have a fair reason for dismissing the employee?

Once the employee has proved that he is within the unfair dismissal legislation and has been dismissed the employer must show that there was a fair reason for the dismissal. Quite often the reason is misconduct, for example disobeying orders, non co-operation, poor time-keeping, drunkenness, violence and swearing, dishonesty, incompetence or other capability problems. Continuing and persistent ill health would be a good example. Another is where it would be illegal for the employee to continue in employment. Finally there may have been some other substantial reason justifying dismissal. The following are particular examples.

Misconduct – disobeying the reasonable instructions of an employer
As already mentioned it is implied that employees will comply with the reasonable instructions and requests of their employer. However, if the requirement is to perform work which is completely beyond the purpose for which the employee was employed in the first place, the employee may be justified in refusing to comply.

In one case several employees had been breaking the disciplinary rules of their employer, a betting shop owner, in that they had placed bets on their own behalf. The employees were dismissed but they claimed compensation for unfair dismissal. It was held by the tribunal that the dismissal was in fact unfair. It was not sufficient that just because the disciplinary rules stated that dismissal would follow a breach of the employer's rules and regulations, that such a dismissal was necessarily fair.

Failure to co-operate
This may occur in a number of ways. In one case the contract of employment stated that an employee would be expected to work as much overtime as was necessary to ensure continuity of production. One employee was usually reluctant to work overtime but was prepared to do so when persuaded. He was subsequently dismissed for failing to work overtime on a specific occasion. His claim for unfair dismissal was rejected because he had failed to comply with a term of his employment.

Poor time-keeping
This will usually be sufficient to constitute a breach of discipline. Usually though an employer would give an employee who was late for work a

specific warning stating that if he did not arrive on time in the future he would be dismissed. However, if an employee was justified in being late but was nonetheless dismissed a tribunal would almost certainly order reinstatement or compensation.

In one case two employees who had been employed for some time with very good work records were absent for a few hours one afternoon without permission and without having informed anyone as to their whereabouts. They were dismissed and claimed compensation but the tribunal decided that as the employees were of sufficient seniority their unexplained absence could not be justified and consequently they had been dismissed fairly.

Drunkenness

The extent to which drunkenness would justify dismissal is one of degree. It will also depend on what kind of job the employee had. Normally an employer would be expected to give an oral or written warning to an employee stating that if there was a repetition of such misbehaviour disciplinary action would be taken.

Violence

This will depend on the gravity of the offence taking into account the seriousness and the circumstances in which it occurred.

Dishonesty

Theft in the workplace is usually sufficient reason to justify summary dismissal but the employer must still behave reasonably and carry out an inquiry. The value of any property taken is not necessarily relevant because dishonesty is dishonesty whatever the amount.

An example of this was a case concerning a young cashier who was operating a till at a check-out. A number of items bought by a customer were missed by the cashier and she was asked to explain why this had happened. She said that she had not been well. The police investigated and the cashier was dismissed although no prosecution was subsequently brought. The cashier claimed unfair dismissal and the tribunal agreed because the cashier had not been given sufficient opportunity to give an explanation.

This case demonstrates that if the proper procedure is not followed the employer will quite likely be liable to pay compensation simply as a result of such failure. Nonetheless it is not necessary for an employer to delay until court proceedings have been completed and for the employee to have been convicted. If the employer has an honest and good reason for believing that the employee has been stealing that in itself may be sufficient to justify dismissal.

It also follows that if a dismissed employee is subsequently acquitted it would not automatically mean that the dismissal was unfair. The rules governing the way in which suspected dishonesty should be dealt with were clarified in a case where the tribunal stated that the simple test is whether the employer had reasonable grounds for thinking that the employee had committed the theft. The same sorts of considerations apply in cases where an employee is suspected of causing damage or vandalising their employer's premises. On the other hand a conviction for a criminal offence, even if it is unrelated to the employee's employment, may nonetheless justify dismissal.

Incapacity, incompetence or lack of qualification

The overriding test in these cases is whether or not the employer has acted reasonably and particularly so in the case where the employee is alleged to be incompetent. It is difficult where an employee is trying hard and doing his best but nonetheless does not come up to scratch. The responsibility is on the employer to try and assist an employee to improve his work performance by additional training and help.

An illustrative example concerned an employee who was employed to manage a non-food depot operated by a company which had other trading activities. The employee was then appointed manager of a food depot operated by the company even though he had not had any previous experience in dealing with this type of work. He was unable to run the depot efficiently and so the employee was offered other employment at a non-food depot as a manager but still at the higher rate of pay that he had been receiving as a food depot manager. The employee refused to take the alternative employment because of inconvenient travel arrangements and he was consequently dismissed. The employee then claimed unfair dismissal but the tribunal considered that the employer had acted reasonably and the employee's claim was therefore rejected. Perhaps not a surprising decision in the circumstances.

Pregnancy

As already mentioned, as a general rule, any dismissal of a female employee who is pregnant is unfair, although to be eligible to make a claim for unfair dismissal she must have worked for the employer for two years. However, apart from being able to claim unfair dismissal a pregnant employee who is dismissed may be able to bring a claim under the Sex Discrimination Act 1975, in which case there is no need for her to have been employed for the two-year period.

This is an area of the law where European Union decisions are beginning to have more and more of an impact. The European Court decision which now enables part-time employees to bring a claim for unfair dismissal after only two years of employment and not five years as before is a good example. One of the reasons for that decision is that part-time workers tend to be women and therefore to make it a requirement that such employees (most of whom would in practice be women) must have been employed for five years before being able to bring a claim for unfair dismissal was discriminatory. However, dismissal for reasons of pregnancy may not be as clear-cut as imagined. In one case a female employee with a bad attendance record had been given various warnings including a final written warning prior to her becoming pregnant. The employee unfortunately suffered a miscarriage and had to go into hospital and the employer sacked her in her absence. The employee claimed unfair dismissal and the tribunal agreed saying that her dismissal was attributable to her miscarriage and was not connected with her previous disciplinary record.

Industrial action

An employee may be sacked as a result of taking strike action or being involved in other industrial action if such action was not authorised. If the strike action has been officially endorsed by the union then it is open to the employer to sack all of those involved but not just some.

Some other substantial reason

It will depend very much on the facts but the principle underlying this reason is that an employer should be able to dismiss an employee in circumstances which justify dismissal and which do not fall into any of the preceding categories.

Was the employer's behaviour reasonable?

This is the last stage in the process. An employer must show that he behaved reasonably in dismissing the employee. If the employer cannot prove that he had a fair reason for dismissing the employee there will not be any need for the tribunal to consider the question of whether the employer behaved reasonably.

In arriving at its decision the tribunal would have to ask itself what a reasonable employer would have done in response to similar facts which gave rise to the dismissal. The question to be asked is whether the decision to terminate the employment was reasonable, or would some other decision have been appropriate in the circumstances. Apart from a situation in which the employee was guilty of gross misconduct entitling the employer to dismiss him summarily the employer must usually have warned the employee (either orally or in writing) as to his future conduct.

There is also the requirement as has already been mentioned to ensure that an employee is given the opportunity to put his case prior to his dismissal. This cannot be emphasised too often because an employer must almost without exception give his employee a fair hearing. This is an important element in carrying out the unfair dismissal procedure correctly and if the employer fails to do so an employee may well succeed in his claim even though other aspects of the case would not justify it. Quite often a tribunal will uphold a claim for unfair dismissal but reduce the amount of an award to reflect the extent to which the employee is considered to have contributed to his dismissal.

10.4 Health and safety at work

Sources of law

There are numerous statutes, codes of practice and regulations which govern health and safety at work. There are two principal sources of law which determine the responsibility of employers for the health and safety of their employees as well as others who may be affected. These are:

- ☐ Common law duties which include taking reasonable care not to subject employees to unnecessary risk, providing a safe place of work, and protecting employees from foreseeable risks of injury.
- ☐ Statutory duties which include those imposed by the Health and Safety at Work Act 1974 (HSWA) and the numerous management of health and safety at work regulations that have followed at what seems to be an increasing rate.

A breach of the common law duty is called a civil wrong and constitutes the tort of negligence. Negligence on the part of an employer would enable an injured employee to institute proceedings in the civil courts claiming damages for the injuries caused by such negligence. Although the HSWA has existed since 1974 the common law principles continue to run in parallel with the 1974 Act and to some extent, confusingly at times, the two overlap.

The HSWA on the other hand imposes only criminal liability. Consequently where an employer is in breach of the 1974 Act which results in injury to an employee, the employer can be prosecuted and fined or exceptionally imprisoned. However, at the same time the employer can also be subject to a claim for damages by the injured employee and evidence of any criminal conviction as a result of the prosecution under the 1974 Act would be admissible in connection with any civil claim for damages brought by the employee.

Common law duties

In a nutshell, the common law duty of an employer is to take reasonable care for the health and safety of his employees and to protect them against any reasonably foreseeable risk of injury. This general requirement can be expressed as a number of specific duties which include:

- ☐ ensuring a safe place of work.
- ☐ providing a safe system of work.
- ☐ providing and maintaining safe plant and equipment.
- ☐ ensuring that staff are competent, properly trained and are adequately instructed and supervised.
- ☐ identifying and guarding against reasonably foreseeable risks of injury.

The Health and Safety at Work Act 1974

The 1974 Act is the main piece of legislation setting out the statutory requirements to be observed and implemented by an employer. The Act specifies the general duties and responsibilities which everyone at work has to obey regardless of the type of work which is being done. Before the 1974 Act there were thirty-two different Acts of Parliament and numerous statutory instruments regulating health and safety at work.

The aim of the 1974 Act is to:

- Secure the health, safety and welfare of employees.
- Protect people apart from those at work against risk to health or safety arising out of or in connection with such work activity.
- Control the keeping and use of explosives or highly inflammable or otherwise dangerous substances and generally to prevent the unlawful acquisition possession and use of such substances.
- Control the emission into the atmosphere of noxious or offensive substances.

An employer's duty to employees

Every employer has a general duty to ensure so far as is *reasonably practicable* the health, safety and welfare of employees at work. It should be noted that the term is 'reasonably practicable' which has been defined by the courts as 'a narrower term than is implicitly possible and which implies a computation to be made by the employer in which the amount of risk is placed on one scale and the sacrifice involved in the measures necessary for averting the risk (whether in money, time or trouble) is placed on the other and that if it is shown that there is a gross disproportion between them and the risk is insignificant in relation to the sacrifice the employer would be absolved of any liability'.

This approach has generally been followed by the courts but a number of other factors have to be taken into account in deciding whether or not an employer has fulfilled his responsibilities and obligations. These are:

- the likelihood of injury.
- the potential seriousness of the injury.
- the obviousness of the danger.
- the cost of prevention.
- the degree of inherent risk.

Under the 1974 Act employers must also as far as is reasonably practicable comply with the following:

- Provide and maintain safe plant and systems of work.
- Take reasonable care to ensure that all equipment, apparatus and machinery are of the correct type for the job and are not dangerous or

defective and that such machinery is properly maintained and is safe to use.
- ☐ Inspect and test plant and equipment regularly and remedy any defects.
- ☐ Ensure that there are safe methods and procedures to carry out the work and that such procedures are in fact followed.
- ☐ Warn staff of any hazards and provide any special equipment or clothing which may be required to carry out the work safely.
- ☐ Ensure arrangements for the safe use, handling, storage and transport of articles and substances and also ensure that all goods and substances are properly and safely handled and transported.
- ☐ Provide all necessary information, instruction training and supervision.
- ☐ Provide adequate training in health and safety matters as well as information and instruction which could involve written procedures, handbooks and rules.
- ☐ Maintain a safe place of work and safe means of access and egress, obvious examples of which are to make sure that floors are not slippery and that work areas are tidy and free of rubbish.
- ☐ Maintain a safe working environment with adequate facilities and arrangements for employees' welfare at work.
- ☐ Ensure that any lighting, heating, ventilation, dust and noise levels are acceptable and are not in breach of any appropriate standards.
- ☐ Provide toilet and washing facilities.
- ☐ Not charge for safety measures. The 1974 Act prohibits an employer from charging employees for anything relating to health and safety including protective clothing or equipment.
- ☐ Publish a safety policy which an employer must do where there are more than five employees. The policy must be in the form of a written statement setting out how the health and safety of the employees will be promoted and describing the organisation and arrangements for putting the policy into practice.

The 1974 Act places responsibility for health and safety on the most senior official of the employing organisation. A number of these requirements can, however, be delegated.

The duties imposed by the 1974 Act have been supplemented by the Management of Health and Safety at Work Regulations 1992 which were the direct result of the European framework directive. The Regulations imposed various obligations on the part of employers as follows:

- ☐ To carry out a risk assessment.
- ☐ To make and record arrangements for the implementation of health and safety measures as a result of the risk assessment.
- ☐ To appoint appropriate individuals to implement arrangements for health and safety.
- ☐ To provide intelligible information and appropriate training for employees.

There are also other specified requirements with regard to the risks to the health and safety of 'new and expectant mothers'.

Employer's duties to people other than employees

The 1974 Act specifies that an employer has a duty to conduct his business and undertaking in such a way, so far as is reasonably practicable, to ensure that people who are *not* in his employment but who *may* be affected by it are not exposed to risks to their health and safety. This obligation extends to visitors, neighbours, passers-by and the employees of any sub-contractors who work on the employer's premises.

Employees' duties

The 1974 Act imposes a duty on all employees while at work:

- To take reasonable care for their own health and safety at work and that of others who may be affected by their acts or omissions.
- To co-operate with their employer or any other person to ensure that the requirements of any relevant statutory provisions are complied with.
- Not intentionally or recklessly to interfere with or misuse anything provided in the interests of health, safety or welfare in pursuance of the relevant statutory provisions.

The role of the Health and Safety Executive

The 1974 Act and the related legislation and regulations are enforced by inspectors employed by the Health and Safety Executive. Their powers include the right:

- To enter and inspect premises.
- To examine and investigate any circumstances and require that the relevant plant or premises be left undisturbed as long as is reasonably necessary to enable examination or investigations to take place.
- To collect information.
- To issue improvement notices which require the employer to remedy contraventions within a specified time.
- To issue prohibition notices which have the effect of stopping specified activities until remedial action has been taken; if the inspector is of the opinion that an article or substance constitutes an imminent danger of causing serious personal injury the inspector may take it and make it harmless or destroy it.
- To bring prosecutions for unsafe practices.

If an employer is convicted of a breach of the health and safety legislation the court may impose a fine on any individual or employer (including a company and any director and by extension a trustee or director/trustee) and the amount of such a fine can be as much as £20,000 in the magistrates court or unlimited in the crown court. In exceptional cases a term of imprisonment can be imposed, particularly where there has been a breach of an improvement or prohibition notice.

The recording of accidents and injuries at work

This aspect is governed by the Reporting of Injuries, Diseases and Dangerous Occurrences Regulations 1995 or RIDDOR for short. These regulations require that particular accidents and ill-health which occur at work must be recorded, notified and then reported by a nominated individual to either the Health and Safety Executive or the local authority environmental health department. Examples of what must be notified include the following:

- ☐ The death of anyone as a result of an accident at work.
- ☐ A major injury suffered as a result of such accident.
- ☐ Any injury suffered by anyone other than an employee as a result of an accident at work.
- ☐ An occurrence which is regarded as dangerous.

In addition, employers have to ensure that all injuries regardless of their extent are recorded in an accident book containing the full name, address and occupation of the injured person, the date and time of the accident, where it happened, the nature of the injury and how it arose and the name, address and occupation of the individual giving the notice if someone other than the injured person.

10.5 Volunteers

Even though volunteers are usually reimbursed their expenses this does not make them employees in the eyes of the law. Consequently a volunteer would not normally have any statutory employment rights and could not, for example, claim compensation for unfair dismissal or be entitled to redundancy pay or maternity pay. A consultant or similar person would be regarded as an independent contractor and would therefore not be an employee.

In 1984 an industrial tribunal ruled that a volunteer who had worked for a charity could not claim compensation for unfair dismissal because the work carried out was not in the course of employment. In a more recent case in 1997 a tribunal decided that a volunteer who received expenses from a charity at a set rate each week, and who continued to do so during periods of holiday or sickness was an employee of that charity.

The distinction between an employee and a volunteer does raise the question as to what liability would attach to a charity (and its trustees if the charity is unincorporated) as a result of the negligence of a volunteer. In practice it is unlikely to create a problem because the charity should be insured, but there could be circumstances in which the consequences of the negligent action of a volunteer would not be covered by insurance in which case the charity and its trustees could be liable to meet a claim for compensation by the injured third party.

As already mentioned, the Health and Safety at Work legislation imposes a duty on an employer to conduct his undertaking in such a way, so far as is reasonably practicable, to ensure that not only employees but people other than employees are not exposed to risks to their health or safety. Although there is as yet no case on this point, it is virtually certain that a volunteer would come within the ambit of this duty and the charity and its trustees could be liable under this legislation as a consequence of any breach.

10.6 Other useful publications

ICSA Publishing publishes:

Burnell, J. *Managing People in Charities* (1997).
Martin, D.M. *Personnel Management* (1991).

NCVO publishes:

Compromising on Quality
Evaluating Training Programmes
Getting into Training
Training for the Voluntary Sector
Equality in Action

HMSO publishes:

Prevention of Illegal Working – Guidance for Employers
Display Screen Equipment at Work
Managing Health and Safety at Work
Work Places: Health and Safety and Welfare

The Industrial Society publishes:

Risk Assessment: A Practical Guide

ACAS publishes a number of guidance leaflets.

11

ACCOUNTING AND FINANCIAL MANAGEMENT

11.1 Financial control and compliance

Responsibility of trustees to maintain financial control

One of the main areas of responsibility of any charity trustee, whether an ordinary trustee or director/trustee is to ensure that the assets and other property of the charity are protected and that such assets are employed in achieving the purposes for which the charity is established. Consequently a charity trustee must ensure that there are adequate internal financial controls governing the way in which the assets of the charity are deployed.

It is also necessary to demonstrate to the supporters and the other constituents of the charity as well as 'the world at large' that the charity is being run in a financially prudent manner – increasingly, public accountability has to be satisfied and those charities which are more successful in demonstrating financial probity and 'value for money' are more likely to attract funds from donors and other supporters. All in all if the confidence of the public is enhanced it can only be of benefit to the charitable sector as a whole.

This chapter is not a detailed treatise on the intricacies of accounting but is intended to deal with the main elements of financial control and the statutory requirements to be met by charities. To that extent therefore this chapter is no more than an overview of the requirements.

Recent changes in the law

A new order has been established as a result of the Charities Act 1993 and the Charities (Accounts and Reports) Regulations 1995. These two pieces of legislation spell out and amplify the responsibilities of trustees in the conduct of financial matters. There is, however, still some divergence between the accounting requirements to be met by an unincorporated charity and a charity which is constituted as a company limited by guarantee. A charitable company must still prepare its accounts in accordance with the provisions of the Companies Acts 1985–89. Charitable companies also have to file copies of their statutory accounts and reports (as required by companies legislation) with the Registrar of Companies.

The SORP

The Statement of Recommended Practice (SORP) which underpins the new legislation applies equally to charitable companies as it does to charities which are not incorporated. The SORP contains recommendations on the way in which a charity is to report annually on the resources which it has at its disposal for its charitable purposes.

The SORP has been approved by the Accounting Standards Board. In the forward to the SORP the Charity Commission confirms that it applies to all charities regardless of their size, constitution or complexity although there are more specialised requirements in the case, for example, of higher educational institutions and registered housing associations.

Financial management control procedures

The onus is on the trustees to establish financial control systems so that they can, as already mentioned, discharge their general responsibilities as trustees effectively. This is not always easy to do because the range of charitable activity is so extensive and it is not possible to say what exactly ought to be included in any particular control system and what its features should be. However some basic principles apply to most charitable organisations however constituted and whatever their charitable activity. These principles are:

- ☐ The formulation of a business plan. Quite often a charity will be established to fulfil a specific purpose, for example to acquire a particular item of medical equipment or to achieve something on a wider basis, for example to provide services for the elderly. A business plan should therefore include among other things the principal objectives which the trustees wish to achieve over a particular time frame. Such a plan should include the estimated income for the period, the cost of the projects to be undertaken, and the capital equipment which is required.
- ☐ The preparation of an annual budget. This should contain more detail than the basic income and expenditure information contained in the business plan.
- ☐ The preparation of management accounts and the exercise of budgetary control. Management accounts need to be prepared and distributed fairly

regularly. Depending on the nature of the charity its management accounts should be either monthly or quarterly. As much information as possible which is important to management should be set out and the actual results compared with budget estimates. Any variances should be noted and explanations provided.

☐ The preparation and consideration of a periodic cashflow summary. This summary should cover the same period as the management accounts and also include any revisions to the forecast for the rest of the budget period. Some unavoidable fixed costs are bound to be incurred and therefore a regular flow of income must self-evidently be generated by the charity in order to meet such fixed costs.

Management audit and the structure of the organisation

Any financial systems which are designed to maintain and measure the effectiveness of internal control must suit the structure of the charity. A plan should be prepared showing the respective areas of responsibility, the various lines of authority and of reporting. All aspects of the charity's activities and administration must be covered by the financial control system so that it is comprehensive and achieves its purpose. No control system however refined or well designed can guarantee that the organisation is immune from the consequences of management failure or, even worse, fraud. Trustees will be very well aware that they may incur personal liability if the charity suffers loss as a result of the misappropriation or misapplication of its funds. The setting up of proper controls should be seen by the trustees not only as protection for themselves but also as the means by which the charity's objectives can be fulfilled. If the trustees are neglectful of their obligations then as already mentioned they may be personally responsible and have to repay the charity the money which has improperly been lost. If, however, the trustees can show that adequate financial controls were in place that would help them to combat any claims of breach of trust against them.

By the nature of their operations and their structure, legal and organisational, charities may be more at risk than commercial undertakings to management failure as well as fraud. Trustees are often people who do not have a great deal of time to spare and cannot be involved in day-to-day management. Any financial control system must include provision for internal checks and balances to be carried out so that any risk of serious error or misappropriation can be minimised. This is especially so in the case of the smaller charity where the work may be carried out largely by volunteers and where there may be only one or two permanent members of staff. Consequently the treasurer of such a charity who is likely to be an honorary treasurer should ideally have the knowledge and experience sufficient to 'do the job' and will need as far as possible to work closely with the management on a day-to-day basis.

One of the more important ways to exercise control is to separate out any aspects or duties which if combined could enable one person to record and process a complete transaction. Consequently if such duties can be separated there is a significant reduction in the scope for errors as well as deliberate manipulation or abuse. Mistakes are also more likely to go unnoticed if one individual is also responsible for checking his own work.

Where a charity is more complex or quite sizeable the introduction of a system of continuous audit of the operations of the charity should be considered. It is very important that the management auditor should be completely independent of other executive functions and should have direct responsibility and access to the chief executive and also if necessary to the chairman of the governing body.

11.2   Management accounting

Basic principles

The trustees should consider all the internal and external information requirements which may have to be met and take these into consideration in devising the accounting system. In some ways relationships in the voluntary sector are more complicated than are to be found in commercial undertakings. Many charities are increasingly providing services in partnership or under agency arrangements where joint budgeting and reporting arrangements have to be agreed. It is often the case that grants are made for specifically defined services and to that extent grants could be regarded as being restricted and therefore care must be exercised to ensure that the money is used only for the purposes agreed with the donor.

Fund accounting is an integral part of the new SORP and therefore in designing and monitoring the financial system trustees need to take into account not only information required by the various stakeholders but also their obligations to those regulatory bodies which may control the whole or part of the charity's activities. In addition there is the requirement to produce a new reporting document for charities in the form of the Statement of Financial Activities (SOFA). The SOFA (which applies to a charity with an annual income in excess of £100,000) requires all charitable expenditure to be analysed on an activity basis which includes both direct costs and a proportion of any support costs attributable to each activity.

Control of funds received as cash

All funds and cash received by a charity through the post should be subject to certain controls, the first being that any income received through the post should be dealt with as quickly as possible and in the presence of two individuals. All incoming cheques and cash should be immediately recorded and the entry verified by someone other than the person who has made the entry which is particularly important so far as cash is concerned. There may be some practical problems in achieving this ideal but it is the procedure which is recommended. In addition it would be sensible if a rota system was introduced for staff involved in opening the post.

Many charities raise large sums of money in cash by means of public collections which may take place either in the street or as a result of house-to-house collections, fund-raising events, sponsorships and other functions. Simple precautions can be taken, for example, collection boxes should be individually numbered and their allocation and return formally controlled. Any collecting box should be sealed so that if it is opened prior to the contents being recorded it would be apparent. Collection boxes which remain in the same place should be opened regularly and two individuals present when the contents are counted. The location of collection boxes should be recorded and a diary kept of how frequently each box is opened. The proceeds of a general public collection should be counted in the presence of the collector and a receipt given and any money collected should be paid directly into the charity's bank or building society account.

House-to-house collections and the like are often organised by volunteers or branches which may not be under the control of the main organisation. It is therefore difficult to ensure sound financial discipline on a comprehensive basis but this must be encouraged as much as possible. Once the cash reaches the charity adequate security must be maintained where at all possible. A large part of general donations and voluntary income is received in cash unsupported by any form of voucher. Considerable care will therefore be required to safeguard against loss for any reason.

Sources of income

Income is derived from various sources. The following are examples:

- ☐ Voluntary income. There is a variety of voluntary fund-raising activities. Some methods have been tried and tested for a long time and consequently there should be some historical data on which to judge the level of future income. Nonetheless, what has happened previously is not necessarily a guide to what can be achieved currently or in the future; perhaps those responsible for collecting funds in previous years are no longer involved. The loss of an experienced fund-raiser, or for that matter a change in economic circumstances generally, will have a significant effect on the amounts of money raised.
- ☐ Statutory grants. Statutory grants may either be for core funding or specific projects in which case such grants will probably be treated as restricted. Grants are usually negotiated for a fixed period, probably

between three and five years. Some caution will be required where grants have to be re-negotiated during a planning period, particularly at times where public expenditure is being constrained.
- [ ] Service agreements. Service agreements are usually for a specific period and it is prudent to be cautious if such an arrangement is to cease during a planning period. Agreement should be reached at the outset as to the way in which terminal costs are to be shared when a project comes to an end and by what means any assets contributed by either or both parties are to be distributed between them.
- [ ] Income from investments and financial activities. The trustees will need to consider what income may be expected from any investments held by the charity and whether any variations in the value of those investments or income derived are expected during the planning period.
- [ ] Income of a capital nature. This may be received from two sources, one being a specific capital appeal and the other a disposal of surplus assets.
- [ ] Legacies. These can be in the form of pecuniary bequest which is a specific amount or a residuary bequest which is share in any assets remaining after all debts and expenses have been met and specific legacies have been paid. A residuary legacy is not always easy to value correctly especially where property or other similar assets are included. The SORP does however require that major bequests be included in the accounts when it is clear that the charity is legally entitled to such a bequest and its value can be calculated with reasonable certainty.

Expenditure on primary charitable objectives

The trustees and senior management should as a matter of course have discussed and agreed the main aims and objectives for the planning period; these will usually be set out in the form of individual projects, each under the control of a project manager if the charity is organised on such a basis. Where the charity employs staff they should be involved in agreeing the way in which expenditure is planned during the period under consideration. Discussion at an early stage should help staff to appreciate the main elements which will have to be monitored to achieve success. There will also need to be an appreciation of the quality standards to be achieved.

Capital funding

Raising funds to meet the running expenses of a charity is clearly an ongoing requirement, but from time to time a charity may need to raise capital for a number of reasons. Capital funding may be required to replace worn out assets, to enhance facilities, to expand the area of work or activity, to fund a new special project, or for endowment, an example of which would be to underwrite the cost of a research programme.

11.3 Annual statutory accounts

Statutory regulations

The statutory requirements to be satisfied in the preparation of a charity's accounts are contained in part VI of the Charities Act 1993 and the Charities (Accounts and Reports) Regulations 1995 which came into force on 1 March 1996.

Financial thresholds

The way in which accounts are prepared depends on the level of income received by charities. The requirements regarding the preparation of the statutory accounts are as follows:

Annual gross income	Accounting basis	External review requirement
Below £10,000	Receipts and payments	None
Above £10,000 but below £100,000	Receipts and payments	Independent examination
Above £100,000 but below £250,000	Accruals	Independent examination
Above £250,000	Accruals	Audit

Regime for charities with an annual income of less than £100,000

A charity with a gross income of less than £100,000 which is not a company is permitted to prepare its accounts on a receipts and payments basis with a statement of its assets and liabilities at the year end instead of preparing full accounts for a particular financial year. The Charity Commission has issued a guide for those charities which decide to prepare their annual accounts on a receipts and payments basis. This provides very helpful advice on those parts of the SORP which may be applicable to smaller charities. There are no statutory requirements as to what must be contained in the receipts and payment account or the statement of assets and liabilities, although the Commission has published a model receipts and payments account and statement of assets and liabilities.

The more important matters which trustees should address in preparing the accounts of their charity are:

- ☐ Disclosure of the accounting basis.
- ☐ Accounting for branches.
- ☐ Materiality.
- ☐ Consistency.

Many charities have funds which are subject to some restriction in the way they may be spent or applied, for example where those funds are subject to a specific condition which means that they have to be spent for a particular purpose. The fact that a condition has been imposed means that such funds are to be treated as restricted. Another example is permanent endowment, which is capital that cannot be used as though it were income. Any income which is derived from restricted funds is itself to be held on the same basis and cannot be used for other purposes of the charity, unless of course the donor has agreed that the income can be used for other purposes.

Regime for charities with an annual income in excess of £100,000

One of the objectives of the new legislation and SORP is to reform the way in which a charity's financial affairs should be presented. The intention is that the accounts should give a view which is true and fair to a greater extent than provided by the previous commercial style of presentation. Another important document in this connection is the SOFA, which combines the old income and expenditure account with a reconciliation and analysis of the movement of funds.

The main provisions of the SORP

The real significance of the SORP will be experienced by charities with a gross income in a financial year which exceeds the current threshold of £100,000. So far as charitable companies are concerned the requirements of the SORP have to be looked at in the light of the requirements of company law and be modified if it is necessary to do so. The accounts of a charitable company will require a separate summary income and expenditure account to be prepared in addition to the SOFA in order to comply with companies legislation. Not only that, but the larger charities will also have to take into account the requirements of any current statements of standard accounting practice and any financial reporting standards.

The annual report

Charity trustees are obliged under the Charities Act 1993 to prepare in respect of each financial year an annual report containing a summary of the activities of their charity during the year. In the case of a charity whose income or expenditure is more than £10,000 the trustees will have to send to the Commission a copy of the annual report with the accounts. Charities whose income or expenditure is less than £10,000 in a year do not have to send an annual report to the Commission unless specifically asked to do so. A narrative section must be included in the report which describes the charity's activities and achievements in the year and must also include the factual information mentioned below.

For smaller charities which are defined for this purpose as those with a gross income of less than £100,000, the only requirement is to provide a brief summary of the main activities and achievements of the charity during the year under review. In the case of a charity with an income of more than £100,000 the report must mention all of its significant activities including any changes and its achievements. If anything has occurred since the end of the year to which the report relates which might affect future activities or developments then mention of this has to be made. A description of the structure of the charity and details of any assets which it holds on behalf of another charity have also to be included.

Every charity must in its annual report include where applicable the following matters:

- ☐ The full name of the charity and any other name which it may use.
- ☐ The registered charity number and company registration number.
- ☐ The registered office if a charitable company and the main address of the charity.
- ☐ An explanation of the charity's objects.
- ☐ The names of the charity trustees which should include the name of any trustee who was in office during the relevant year.

11.4 Statutory audit or independent examination

The new regime

The new legal requirements are, as already mentioned, contained in part VI of the Charities Act 1993 and the regulations made under the 1993 Act. Again it is unfortunate that there are anomalies between the requirements to be met by an unincorporated charity and a charitable company because as noted the various thresholds are not compatible between the two sources of legislation. The following is a summary of the requirements:

Gross annual income	*Incorporated charity*		*Unincorporated charity*	
	Audit	Audit exemption report	Audit	Independent examination
Less than £10,000	No	No	No	No
£10,001–£90,000	No	No	No	Yes
£90,001–£250,000	No	Yes	No	Yes
over £250,000	Yes	No	Yes	No

Auditors and independent examiners

Charitable companies which require a statutory audit to be undertaken must appoint an approved qualified practitioner. The 1993 Act requires that both a charitable company and an unincorporated charity whose total annual income exceeds £250,000 in its financial year must arrange for their accounts to be audited by a person who is eligible for appointment as a company auditor or is a member of a body for the time being specified in the regulations contained in the 1993 Act. Once the charity's income exceeds £250,000 in a year the full audit requirement will continue for the next following two years even if its income falls below £250,000 in each of those two years.

If an unincorporated charity's total annual income is less than £250,000 the charity's trustees may elect that the accounts be examined by an independent examiner who is defined as 'an independent person who is reasonably believed by the trustees to have the requisite ability and practical experience to carry out a competent examination of the accounts'.

Audit requirements of charitable companies

The audit or exemption report requirements in respect of charitable companies are broadly similar to those for other companies, apart from the fact that the exemption report threshold for a charitable company is £90,000 gross income rather than turnover and the audit threshold is £250,000 gross income and not £350,000 turnover. However, charitable companies also have to abide by charity law generally and if the charity is also registered it will in addition have to file an annual report and its own full set of statutory accounts with the Charity Commission where the income *or* expenditure is greater than £10,000 or if less, when specifically requested by the Commission to do so. The requirements in respect of the annual report of a charitable company to be submitted to the Commission are as laid down in the 1993 Act, as amplified from time to time by the Commission.

Audit requirements in a charity's governing document

It is very often the case that the governing document of a charity will specify that an audit must be carried out. On the face of it such a requirement would override the more modest requirement applicable to charities with an income of less than £250,000 which depending on their level of income can either have their accounts independently examined or if less than £10,000, not examined at all. If the governing document requires the accounts to be audited then an annual audit must be conducted regardless of what the regulations say.

11.5 Other Useful Publications

The Charity Commission publishes:

CC8   Internal Financial Controls for Charities
CC51 Charity Accounts: The New Framework
CC52 Charity Accounts: Charities Under the £10,000 Threshold
CC53 Charity Accounts: Charities Over the £10,000 Threshold
CC54 Accounting for the Smaller Charity
CC55 Accruals Accounting for the Smaller Charity
CC56 The Carrying Out of an Independent Examination
Accounting by Charities – Statement of Recommended Practice

ICSA Publishing publishes:

The Charities Manual
Manley, K. *Financial Management for Charities and Voluntary Organisations* (1994)
Randall, A. *A Practical Guide to SORP and the Regulations* (1997)
Wise, D. *Performance Measurement for Charities* (1995)

Other:

The Charities (Accounts and Reports) Regulations (1995) HMSO

APPENDIX 1

MODEL FORM OF CONSTITUTION OF AN UNINCORPORATED CHARITABLE ASSOCIATION

Note: In Appendices 1 and 2 square brackets denote text which is either an example or is optional and where blank requires completion.

Name
1. The name of the Association (the 'Charity') is

Objects
2. The Charity is established to [relieve need and hardship of the wives, former wives, husbands, former husbands, family, widows, widowers, children and other dependants of the members and former members of – define]

Powers
3. In furtherance of the said objects, but not further or otherwise the Charity shall have the following powers:
   (a) [to provide, maintain and conduct treatment and training centres, day and residential services and employment centres].
   (b) [to promote, maintain and extend a network of individuals to develop and improve advisory services].
   (c) to collect and disseminate information relating to the objects of the Charity and exchange such information with other bodies having similar objects and specifically, but not exclusively:
   (i) to bring together representatives of voluntary organisations, government departments, statutory authorities and individuals.

(ii) to provide evidence for government and public enquiries.
(iii) to cause to be written, printed, or to be put on computer disk or otherwise originated and reproduced, and republished or circulated (whether gratuitously or not), any newspapers, periodicals, magazines, or books, pamphlets, leaflets or other documents, or films or recorded tapes (whether audio or visual or both).
(iv) to arrange and provide for or join in arranging and providing for the holding of exhibitions, meetings, lectures, classes, seminars and training courses.

(d) to establish and support or aid in the establishment and support of any charitable associations and to subscribe or guarantee money for charitable purposes in any way connected with the objects of the Charity or calculated to further its objects.

(e) to raise funds by any lawful means including personal or written appeals public meetings or otherwise as may be deemed expedient for the purpose of raising funds and obtaining contributions to the funds of the Charity in the form of donations, annual subscriptions or otherwise and for that purpose to appoint collectors and volunteers as may be considered expedient PROVIDED that the Charity shall not undertake any permanent trading activities to raise funds for its objects.

(f) to promote research, experimental work, scientific investigation and development into any aspect of the objects of the Charity and its work and to disseminate the useful results of any such research for the public benefit.

(g) to accept any gifts, subscriptions (whether or not under a deed of covenant), donations, bequests or devises of land, monies, securities or other real or personal property.

(h) to purchase, take on lease or by exchange, hire or otherwise acquire any real or personal property and any rights or privileges necessary for the promotion of the objects of the Charity, and to construct maintain and alter any buildings necessary or convenient for the work of the Charity.

(i) subject to such consents as may be required by law, to manage, mortgage, sell, dispose of or otherwise deal with all or any part of the property of the Charity.

(j) to draw, make, accept, endorse, discount, execute and issue promissory notes, bills of exchange, cheques and other instruments, and to operate bank accounts in the name of the Charity.

(k) subject to such consents as may be required by law to borrow and raise money in such manner and to give and provide security as may be thought fit.

(l) to take and accept any gift of money, property or other assets, whether subject to any special trust or not for any one or more of the objects of the Charity.

(m) to invest the monies of the Charity not immediately required for its purposes in or upon such investments, securities or property as may be thought fit, subject nevertheless to such conditions (if any) and such consents (if any) as may for the time being be imposed or required by law.

(n)   to provide financial assistance, to make grants and donations to and to provide equipment and apparatus for the furtherance of the objects of the Charity.

(o)   to pay out of the funds of the Charity the cost of any premium of any insurance or indemnity to cover the liability of the members of the Committee (or any of them) which by virtue of any rule of law would otherwise attach to them in respect of any negligence, default or wrongful omission, breach of duty or breach of trust of which they may be guilty in relation to the charity PROVIDED that any such insurance or indemnity shall not extend to any claim arising from wilful fraud or wrongdoing or default on the part of the Committee (or any of them).

(p)   to engage, employ and remunerate any agents or employees to supervise, organise and carry out the work of the Charity and to make all reasonable and necessary provision for the payment of pensions and superannuation to or on behalf of employees former employees and their widows and other dependants.

(q)   to subscribe to, support, affiliate, become a member of, amalgamate with or co-operate with any other charitable organisation, institution, society or body not formed for or established for purposes of profit whose objects are wholly or in part similar to those of the Charity and which by its constitution prohibits the distribution of its income and property amongst its members to an extent at least as great as is imposed on the Charity.

(r)   to establish where necessary local branches (whether autonomous or not).

(s)   to do all such other lawful things as shall further the attainment of the objects of the Charity.

Membership

4. Membership shall be open to any individual or organisation who is interested in furthering the objects of the Charity and who completes an application form as prescribed by the Committee but the number of members shall not fall below [three].

5. The Committee shall have the right for good and sufficient reason to reject an application for membership.

6. Members of the Charity may be required to pay an annual subscription of such amount and on such date as may be determined from time to time by the Charity in General Meeting and the failure by a member to pay such subscription may render him liable to be excluded from membership of the Charity. Any member may by a unanimous resolution of the Committee be exempted from payment of the annual subscription. Any such exempted member shall be known as an honorary member and shall have all the rights of a member.

7. No paid employee whether in full-time or part-time employment of the Charity shall be eligible for membership of the Charity or the Committee.

8. If not less than seventy-five per cent of the members of the Committee present at a meeting so resolve, the Committee shall have the right for good and sufficient reason to terminate the membership of any member PROVIDED that the member shall have the right to be heard by the Committee before a final decision is made.

General meetings

9. The Charity shall in each year hold an Annual General Meeting at such time and place as the Committee shall determine. Not more than fifteen months shall elapse between the date of one Annual General Meeting and that of the next.

10. The business of the Annual General Meeting shall include:
    (a) the election of members of the Committee.
    (b) the appointment of an auditor or independent examiner.
    (c) consideration of the report of the Committee on the previous year's activity and the audited or examined financial statements.
    (d) consideration of any resolution proposed by the Committee or on the requisition of not less than [five] per cent of the members of the Charity having the right to vote at an Annual General Meeting provided that such requisition is received by the secretary not less than [forty-two] days before the meeting.

11. The Committee shall within [twenty-one] days of receiving a request signed by not less than [ten] per cent of the members and stating the purpose of the request call an Extraordinary General Meeting of the Charity.

12. Such Extraordinary General Meeting shall be held within [thirty-five] days of the receipt of the request.

Notice of general meetings

13. At least twenty-one clear days' notice of each Annual General Meeting and fourteen clear days' notice of an Extraordinary General Meeting shall be given in writing to each member together with details of the business to be discussed, PROVIDED that accidental failure to notify any member shall not invalidate the meeting; PROVIDED also that a General Meeting called at shorter notice shall be deemed to have been duly called if so agreed:
    (a) if an Annual General Meeting by all members entitled to attend and vote thereat.
    (b) in any other cases by not less than ninety-five per cent of all members entitled to attend and vote thereat.

Proceedings at general meetings

14. No business shall be transacted at any General Meeting unless a quorum is present. The quorum at any General Meeting shall be [one-third]

of the total membership of the Charity or such other number not less than [three] as the Charity may from time to time determine in General Meeting.
15. If within thirty minutes from the time appointed for a meeting a quorum is not present or during a meeting a quorum ceases to be present, the meeting shall stand adjourned to the same day in the next week at the same time and place or at such other time and place as the Committee may determine.
16. The chairman of the Committee shall preside as chairman at every General Meeting and if the chairman is not present within fifteen minutes after the time appointed for holding the meeting or is unwilling to preside, the members present shall choose some member of the Committee or if no such member is present and willing to take the chair they shall choose some other member present to preside.

Votes of members
17. At any General Meeting a resolution put to the vote of the meeting shall be decided on a show of hands unless before or upon the declaration of the result of the show of hands a poll be demanded by the chairman or by at least [five] members present in person or by proxy. A poll so demanded shall be taken at such time and place and in such manner as the chairman shall direct and the result of the poll shall be deemed to be the resolution of the meeting at which the poll was demanded. A demand for a poll may be withdrawn.
18. Votes may be given on a show of hands or on a poll, either personally or by proxy, provided that on a show of hands every person entitled to vote whether as member or as proxy shall have one vote only, however many proxies he holds.
19. In the case of an equality of votes, whether on a show of hands or on a poll, the chairman of a meeting shall be entitled to a casting vote in addition to any other vote he may have.
20. A proxy shall be appointed in writing by instrument signed by the appointor and delivered to the office specified in the notice convening the meeting not less than forty-eight hours before the time for holding the meeting. The instrument appointing a proxy shall be deemed to confer authority to demand or join in demanding a poll.
21. A resolution in writing signed by all members for the time being entitled to receive notice of and to attend and vote at General Meetings shall be as valid and effective as if the same had been passed at a General Meeting duly convened and held.

Powers and duties of the committee
22. The affairs and property of the Charity shall be controlled and managed by a management committee ('the Committee') which may exercise all such powers of the Charity as are not required by this Constitution to be exercised by the Charity in General Meeting. In particular the Committee shall:

(a) control the admission to and termination of membership of the Charity in accordance with the provisions of Clause 8;
(b) make and vary regulations for the conduct of the affairs of the Charity including the conduct and recording of meetings;
(c) submit to the Annual General Meeting a report together with the audited or examined accounts of the Charity for the immediately preceding financial year;
(d) make and vary regulations for the establishment of local branches as may be necessary and appropriate.

Appointment and retirement of committee members

23. Unless otherwise determined by the Charity in General Meeting, the Committee shall consist of not less than [five] nor more than [fifteen] members. All members of the Charity and any other person who is willing to become a member shall be eligible for election to the Committee.

24. At each Annual General Meeting [one-third] of the members of the Committee or the number nearest to [one-third] shall retire, but shall retain office until the end of the meeting. The retiring members shall be those who have been longest in office since their last election but as between members who have been in office the same length of time those to retire shall (unless they otherwise agree amongst themselves) be decided by lot. A retiring member shall be eligible for re-election [save that a member of the Committee retiring after a period of continuous service of [five] years shall not be eligible for re-election until the Annual General Meeting next after the one at which he retires].

25. The Charity may at an Annual General Meeting fill any vacancies in the Committee.

26. Nominations for members of the Committee signed by a member of the Charity and by the person nominated to indicate his willingness to serve must be received by the chairman at least [fourteen] days before the Annual General Meeting provided that if no nomination is so received for any vacancy a nomination made at the Annual General Meeting for the vacancy shall be valid.

27. The Committee may from time to time appoint a member, or person willing to become a member, of the Charity as a member of the Committee to fill a casual vacancy or by way of addition to the Committee provided that the prescribed maximum is not exceeded. Any member so appointed shall retain his office only until the end of the next Annual General Meeting.

28. The Committee may from time to time co-opt up to [five] members or persons willing to become members of the Charity as additional members of the Committee and notwithstanding that the prescribed maximum is exceeded PROVIDED that the number of co-opted members shall not exceed [one-third] of the total number of members of the Committee in accordance with Clause 23. Co-opted members shall be entitled to vote at meetings of the Committee. They shall hold office only until the end of the next Annual

General Meeting when they shall cease to be members of the Committee but may at the discretion of the Committee subject to the provisions of this clause be co-opted for a further period of service.

No conflict of interest
29. No member of the Committee or any other committee appointed by the Committee shall supply or be directly interested in the supply of goods or services to the Charity except by way of free gift or on a basis which shows no profit or gain directly or indirectly to the member concerned, PROVIDED that this clause shall not apply to
(a) the repayment to members of the Committee or of any committee appointed under Clause 34 of reasonable out-of-pocket expenses;
(b) a member who holds not more than [one] per cent of the capital of a company supplying goods or services to the Charity;
(c) a member who is an official of a bank at which funds of the Charity are deposited;
(d) a member who prior to his election or appointment was already carrying on the business of supplying goods or services to the Charity at a price not exceeding the fair market price and on normal trade terms; but the member shall absent himself from any meeting during the discussion of such business and shall refrain from voting on the matter.

Proceedings of the committee
30. The Committee may regulate its meetings as it thinks fit but shall hold at least [four] meetings a year and not more than [five] months shall elapse between the date of one meeting and the next.
31. A meeting of the Committee at which a quorum is present shall be competent to exercise all the powers vested in the Committee generally. [One-third] of the membership shall be a quorum subject to a minimum of [three].
32. The chairman of the Committee (or in his absence the vice-chairman) shall be entitled to preside at all meetings but if at any meeting neither the chairman nor the vice-chairman is present within five minutes of the appointed time, or if present is unwilling to preside, the members of the Committee present shall choose one of their number to be chairman of the meeting.
33. The proceedings of the Committee shall not be invalidated by any failure to elect or any defect in the election, appointment, co-option, qualification or continuance in office of any member.
34. The Committee may at any time delegate any of its powers to sub-committees whether executive, standing or ad hoc and may make the necessary appointments and regulations for their proceedings. Subject to any such regulations any sub-committee so appointed (which may include persons other than Committee members) shall conform generally to the regulations herein for the proceedings of the Committee. Any such

sub-committee shall report all acts and proceedings to the Committee as soon as possible and shall incur expenditure only within a budget approved by the Committee or with special prior approval of the Committee.

35. A resolution in writing signed by all the members for the time being of the Committee shall be as valid and effectual as if it had been passed at a meeting of the Committee duly convened held and constituted. Any such resolution may consist of several documents in the like form each signed by one or more of the members of the Committee or may be approved by letter, signed by the member or members giving approval.

36. Any member of the Committee who is absent from [three] consecutive meetings of the Committee or who is disqualified by law from acting as a trustee shall automatically cease to be a member of the Committee.

37. The Committee shall keep written minutes of its meetings.

Local branches

38. The Committee may establish local branches for the furtherance of the objects of the Charity. Each branch so established shall act in pursuance of the objects and the policy of the Charity and shall conform to any rules and regulations that may from time to time be laid down by the Committee.

Trust property

39. The Committee may appoint a custodian trustee or not less than [two] or more than [four] individual trustees to hold any property of the Charity subject to the directions of the Committee, and may at any time discharge any custodian trustee or individual trustee so appointed and may at any time appoint one or more additional trustees provided that the prescribed maximum number is not exceeded.

Accounts and audit

40. The income and property of the Charity shall be applied solely towards the promotion and furtherance of its objects.

41. The Committee shall cause such proper accounting records to be kept as necessary to give a true and fair view of the affairs of the Charity and to explain the transactions relating to its assets and liabilities and its income and expenditure. The books of account shall be kept at   or at such other place or places as the Committee shall think fit and shall always be open to the inspection of the members of the Committee.

42. The accounts shall be audited at least once a year by a duly qualified and registered auditor appointed at the Annual General Meeting or so long as the income or expenditure of the Charity does not exceed the appropriate threshold, examined by an independent examiner. The financial year shall end on   in each year. An audited or examined statement of the accounts for the last financial year shall be submitted by the Committee to the Annual General Meeting.

43. A bank account shall be opened and maintained in the name of the Charity with such bank as the Committee shall from time to time decide. Such account shall be under the control of the Committee which shall provide for its method of operation but so that the signatures of at least two members of the Committee, one of whom shall be either the treasurer or the chairman, shall at all times be required.

44. All funds of the Charity shall immediately on receipt be paid into the bank account.

45. The Committee shall make to the best of its ability and enforce adequate regulations for internal control and the security and safe custody of all monies, securities and other documents belonging to the Charity or to any person for whom the Charity has responsibility.

Investments

46. The Committee shall have power from time to time to appoint on such terms (including provision for reasonable remuneration) as the Committee shall at its discretion think fit any person or persons who the Committee reasonably believes to be qualified by his ability in the practical experience of financial matters to be the Charity's investment adviser for the purpose of advising the Committee in relation to the investments of the Charity and managing such investments. The Committee may make such arrangement as it thinks fit for any investments of the Charity or income from those investments to be held by a corporate body as the Charity's nominee and pay reasonable and proper remuneration to any corporate body acting as such nominee.

In making such arrangements as are described above the Committee shall ensure that:

(a) the terms of any delegation of power are clearly stated in writing and contain adequate control mechanisms and

(b) such delegation extends only to such things as the Committee has power to do and

(c) the terms of any such delegation are strictly enforced by the Committee.

Alterations to the constitution

47. This Constitution may be amended only at an Annual General Meeting or an Extraordinary General Meeting of the Charity duly convened and held. Notice of the meeting shall specify the alterations to be proposed. The assent of not less than [seventy-five] per cent of the members of the Charity for the time being present and voting in person or by proxy shall be required to give effect to any alteration PROVIDED that no alteration shall be made to Clause 2, Clauses 50 and 51 or this Clause without the prior consent of the Charity Commissioners PROVIDED also that no alterations shall be made to this Constitution which would cause the Charity to cease to be a charity at law.

Indemnity

48. Every member of the Committee or any other committee and every officer and employee of the Charity shall be entitled to be indemnified out of the assets of the Charity against all losses and liabilities incurred by him or in relation to the execution of his office provided that nothing in this Clause shall entitle him to any indemnity against liability arising through negligence or fraud or similar actions on his part.

Notices

49. Any notice may be given by the Charity to any member either personally or by sending it through the post in a prepaid letter addressed to such member at his last known address in the United Kingdom and any letter so sent shall be deemed to have been received within forty-eight hours of posting.

Dissolution

50. The Charity may be dissolved only by resolution of a majority of [seventy five] per cent of members present and voting in person or by proxy at a General Meeting called at not less than twenty-one days' notice stating the terms of the resolution to be proposed.

51. Upon the dissolution of the Charity any assets remaining after the satisfaction of any proper debts or liabilities shall not be paid to or distributed amongst the members of the Charity but shall be given or transferred [subject to the approval of] to such other charitable institution or institutions having objects similar to the Charity as the Committee may determine.

APPENDIX 2

MODEL FORM OF MEMORANDUM AND ARTICLES OF ASSOCIATION OF A CHARITABLE COMPANY

COMPANIES ACTS 1985 AND 1989

COMPANY LIMITED BY GUARANTEE AND NOT HAVING A SHARE CAPITAL

MEMORANDUM OF ASSOCIATION OF

1. The name of the Charity ('the Company') is
2. The registered office of the Company will be situated in England.
3. The Company's objects are
[to promote any charitable purposes for the benefit of the community in the district of   ('the area of benefit') and, in particular, the advancement of education, the protection of health and the relief of poverty, distress and sickness, and in the furtherance of the said purposes to promote and organise co-operation in the achievement of the same and to that end to bring together representatives of the voluntary organisations and statutory authorities within the area of benefit.]
In furtherance of the said objects, but not further or otherwise, the Company shall have power:
   (a)   to establish and support or aid in the establishment and support of any charitable associations and to subscribe or guarantee money for charitable purposes in any way connected with the objects of the Company or calculated to further its objects;
   (b)   to raise funds and invite and receive contributions from any person or persons whatsoever by way of subscription or donation;

(c) to cause to be written, printed or to be put on computer disk or otherwise reproduced and circulated, gratuitously or otherwise, periodicals, magazines, books, leaflets or other documents or films or recorded tapes;

(d) to hold exhibitions, meetings, lectures, classes, seminars, workshops, conferences and courses either alone or with others;

(e) to promote research, experimental work, scientific investigation and development into any aspect of the objects of the Company and its work and to disseminate the useful results of any such research for the public benefit;

(f) to co-operate and enter into arrangements with any authorities, national, local or otherwise;

(g) to accept subscriptions, donations, devises and bequests of and to purchase, take on lease or in exchange, hire or otherwise acquire and hold any real or personal estate and to maintain and alter any of the same as are necessary for any of the objects of the Company and (subject to such consents as may be required by law) sell, lease or otherwise dispose of or mortgage any such real or personal estate;

(h) to issue appeals, hold public meetings and take such other steps as may be required for the purpose of procuring or encouraging contributions to the funds of the Company in the form of donations, subscriptions or otherwise;

(i) to draw, make, accept, endorse, discount, execute and issue promissory notes, bills of exchange, cheques and other instruments, and to operate bank accounts in the name of the Company;

(j) subject to such consents as may be required by law, to borrow and raise money for the objects of the Company on such terms and conditions and to give and provide such security as may be thought fit;

(k) to carry on trade in so far as either the trade is exercised in the actual carrying out of a primary object of the Company or such trade as is temporary and ancillary to the carrying out of the said objects;

(l) to take and accept any gift of money, property or other assets, whether subject to any special trust or not, for any one or more of the objects of the Company;

(m) to subscribe for either absolutely or conditionally or otherwise acquire shares, stocks, debentures, debenture stock or other securities or obligations of any other company;

(n) to invest the moneys of the Company not immediately required for its objects in or upon such investments, securities or property as may be thought fit, subject nevertheless to such conditions (if any) and such consents (if any) as may be imposed or required by law and subject also as hereinafter provided;

(o) to make any charitable donation either in cash or assets for the furtherance of the objects of the Company;

(p) to collect money on behalf of third parties in particular governmental agencies and to distribute the same to those entitled and to hold funds, property real or otherwise on behalf of any other charitable association or organisation which has similar objects to those of the Company and to charge reasonable sums by way of interest or management costs;

(q) to lend money and give credit, but only in the short term and to take security for such loans or credit and to guarantee or give security for the performance of contracts or obligations by any person or company as may be necessary for the work of the Company;

(r) to pay out of the funds of the Company the cost of any premium of any insurance or indemnity to cover the liability of members of the Committee (or any of them) which by virtue of any rule of law would otherwise attach to them in respect of any negligence, default or wrongful omission, breach of duty or breach of trust of which they may be guilty in relation to the Company PROVIDED that any such insurance or indemnity shall not extend to any claim arising from willful fraud or wrongdoing or default on the part of the Committee (or any of them);

(s) to employ and pay any person or persons not being members of the Committee to supervise, organise, carry on the work of and advise the Company;

(t) to insure and arrange insurance cover for and to indemnify its officers, employees and voluntary workers and those of its members from and against all such risks incurred in the course of the performance of their duties as may be thought fit; and also to arrange fidelity insurance and also insurance to meet any claims arising out of negligent advice;

(u) to pay, subject to the provisions of Clause 4 hereof, reasonable annual sums or premiums for or towards the provision of pensions for officers or employees for the time being of the Company and their dependants;

(v) to apply monies in insuring any buildings or other property to their full value;

(w) to amalgamate with any companies, institutions, societies or associations which are charitable at law and have objects altogether or mainly similar to those of the Company and prohibit the payment of any dividend or profit to and the distribution of any other of their assets amongst their members at least to the same extent as such payments or distributions are prohibited in the case of members of the Company by this Memorandum of Association;

(x) to pay out of the funds of the Company the costs, charges and expenses of and incidental to the formation and registration of the Company;

(y) to establish where necessary local branches (whether autonomous or not);

(z) to do all such other lawful things as shall further the above objects or any of them.

4. The income and property of the Company shall be applied solely towards the promotion of its objects as set forth in this Memorandum of

Association and no portion thereof shall be paid or transferred, directly or indirectly, by way of dividend, bonus or otherwise howsoever by way of profit, to members of the Company and no member of its Committee shall be appointed to any office of the Company paid by salary or fees or receive any remuneration or other benefit in money or money's worth from the Company.

PROVIDED that nothing herein shall prevent any payment in good faith by the Company:

(a) of reasonable and proper remuneration to any member, officer or employee of the Company, not being a member of its Committee, for any services rendered to the Company;

(b) of interest on money lent by any member of the Company or of its Committee at a rate per annum not exceeding [two] per cent less than the minimum lending rate prescribed for the time being by a clearing bank selected by the Committee or [three] per cent whichever is the greater;

(c) of reasonable and proper rent for premises demised or let by any member of the Company or of its Committee;

(d) of fees, remuneration or other benefit in money or money's worth to a company of which a member of the Committee may be a member holding not more than one per cent of the capital of that company;

(e) to any member of its Committee of reasonable out-of-pocket expenses;

(f) of reasonable and proper premiums of insurance or indemnity to cover the liabilities of the Committee (or any of them) effected in accordance with the power contained in Clause 3 (t) hereof.

5. The liability of the members is limited.

6. Every member of the Company undertakes to contribute to the assets of the Company, in the event of the same being wound up while he is a member, or within one year after he ceases to be a member, for payment of the debts and liabilities of the Company contracted before he ceases to be a member, and of the costs, charges and expenses of winding up, and for the adjustment of the rights of the contributories among themselves, such amount as may be required not exceeding [one pound].

7. If upon the winding up or dissolution of the Company there remains, after the satisfaction of all its debts and liabilities, any property whatsoever, the same shall not be paid to or distributed among the members of the Company, but shall be given or transferred to some other charitable institution or institutions having objects similar to the objects of the Company, and which shall prohibit the distribution of its or their income and property to an extent at least as great as is imposed on the Company under or by virtue of Clause 4 hereof, such institution or institutions to be determined by the members of the Company at or before the time of dissolution, and in so far as effect cannot be given to such provision, then to some other charitable object PROVIDED that so far as is practicable the implementation of this clause shall be restricted to the area of benefit.

THE COMPANIES ACTS 1985 AND 1989

COMPANY LIMITED BY GUARANTEE AND NOT HAVING A SHARE CAPITAL

ARTICLES OF ASSOCIATION OF

Interpretation

1. In these Articles:

'the Act' means the Companies Act 1985 as amended by the Companies Act 1989 or any re-enactment or statutory modification of those Acts.

'clear days' in relation to the period of a notice means the period excluding the day when the notice is given or deemed to be given, and the day for which it is given or on which it is to take effect.

'the Committee' means the Management Committee of the Company.

'the Company' means the above named Company.

'the Office' means the registered office of the Company.

'the seal' means the common seal of the Company.

'secretary' means any person appointed to perform the duties of the secretary of the Company.

'the United Kingdom' means Great Britain and Northern Ireland.

Expressions referring to writing shall, unless the contrary intention appears, be construed as including references to printing, lithography, photography, and other modes of representing or reproducing words in a visible form.

Unless the context otherwise requires, words or expressions contained in these Articles shall bear the same meaning as in the Act or any statutory modification thereof in force at the date at which these Articles become binding on the Company.

Words importing the masculine gender shall include the feminine gender and words importing persons shall include corporations.

Objects

2. The Company is established for the objects stated in the Memorandum of Association.

Members

3. The subscribers to the Memorandum of Association and such other persons as the Committee shall admit to membership shall be members of the Company.

4. Every person admitted to membership of the Company shall either sign a written consent to become a member or sign the register of members.

5. An application for membership may be approved or rejected by the Committee. The Committee shall have the right for good and sufficient reason to terminate the membership of any member PROVIDED that the member concerned shall have a right to be heard by the Committee before a final decision is made.

6. Unless the members of the Committee or the Company in General Meeting shall make other provision pursuant to the powers contained in Article 79 the members of the Committee may in their absolute discretion permit any member of the Company to retire provided that after such retirement the number of members is not less than [three].

General meetings
7. The Company shall each year hold a General Meeting as its Annual General Meeting in addition to any other meeting in that year, and shall specify the meeting as such in the notices calling it; and not more than fifteen months shall elapse between the date of one Annual General Meeting of the Company and that of the next. PROVIDED that so long as the Company holds its first Annual General Meeting within eighteen months of its incorporation, it need not hold it in the year of its incorporation or in the following year. The Annual General Meeting shall be held at such time and place as the Committee shall appoint. All General Meetings other than Annual General Meetings shall be called Extraordinary General Meetings.
8. The Committee may, whenever they think fit, convene an Extraordinary General Meeting, and Extraordinary General Meetings shall also be convened on such requisition, or, in default, may be convened by such requisitionists, as provided by section 368 of the Act. If at any time there are not within the United Kingdom sufficient members of the Committee to form a quorum, any member of the Committee or any [two] members of the Company may convene an Extraordinary General Meeting.

Notice of general meetings
9. An Annual General Meeting and a meeting called for the passing of a special resolution shall be called by at least twenty-one clear days' notice in writing. Other meetings shall be called by at least fourteen clear days' notice in writing. The notice shall specify the place, the day and the hour of meeting and, in the case of special business, the general nature of that business, and shall be given, in manner hereinafter mentioned or in such other manner, if any, as may be prescribed by the Company in General Meeting, to such persons as are, under the Articles of the Company, entitled to receive such notices from the Company:
PROVIDED that a meeting of the Company shall, notwithstanding that it is called by shorter notice than that specified in this Article, be deemed to have been duly called if it is so agreed:
    (a) in the case of the Annual General Meeting, by all the members entitled to attend and vote; and
    (b) in the case of any other meeting, by a majority of the members having a right to attend and vote at the meeting, being a majority together representing not less than ninety-five per cent of the total voting rights at that meeting of all the members.

10. The accidental omission to give notice of a meeting to, or the non-receipt of notice of a meeting by, any person entitled to receive notice shall not invalidate the proceedings of that meeting.

Proceedings at general meetings

11. The business to be transacted at an Annual General Meeting shall include the consideration of the accounts, balance sheets, and the reports of the Committee and auditors, the election of members of the Committee in the place of those retiring and the appointment of, and the fixing of the remuneration of, the auditors.

12. No business shall be transacted at any General Meeting unless a quorum of members is present at the time when the meeting proceeds to business; [three] members present in person or [one-tenth] of the membership, whichever is the greater, shall be a quorum. If within thirty minutes from the time appointed for the meeting a quorum is not present, the meeting shall be adjourned to the same day in the next week at the same time and place, or to such other day and at such other time and place as the Committee may determine.

13. The chairman, if any, of the Committee shall chair every General Meeting of the Company, or if there is no such chairman, or if he shall not be present within five minutes after the time appointed for the holding of the meeting or is unwilling to act, the members of the Committee present shall elect one of their number to chair the meeting.

14. If at any meeting no member of the Committee is willing to act as chairman or if no member of the Committee is present within fifteen minutes after the time appointed for holding the meeting, the members present shall choose one of their number to chair the meeting.

15. A member of the Committee shall, notwithstanding that he is not a member of the Company, be entitled to attend and speak at any General Meeting.

16. The chairman may, with the consent of any meeting at which a quorum is present (and shall if so directed by the meeting), adjourn the meeting from time to time and from place to place, but no other business shall be transacted at any adjourned meeting other than the business left unfinished at the meeting from which the adjournment took place. When a meeting is adjourned for fourteen days or more, notice of the adjourned meeting shall be given as in the case of an original meeting. Otherwise it shall not be necessary to give any notice of an adjournment or of the business to be transacted at an adjourned meeting.

17. At any General Meeting a resolution put to the vote of that meeting shall be decided on a show of hands unless a poll is (before or on the declaration of the result of the show of hands) demanded:
   (a) by the chairman; or
   (b) by at least [five] members present in person or by proxy and having the right to vote at the meeting; or

(c) by any member or members present in person or by proxy and representing not less than [one-third] of the total voting rights of all the members having the right to vote at the meeting.

Unless a poll is so demanded, a declaration by the chairman that a resolution has on a show of hands been carried or carried unanimously, or by a particular majority, or lost and an entry to that effect in the book containing the minutes of the proceedings of the Company shall be conclusive evidence of the fact without proof of the number or proportion of the votes recorded in favour of or against such resolution. The demand for a poll may be withdrawn before the poll is taken, but only with the consent of the chairman. The withdrawal of the demand for a poll shall not invalidate the result of a show of hands declared before the demand for the poll was made.

18. In the case of an equality of votes, whether on a show of hands or on a poll, the chairman of the meeting shall be entitled to a second or casting vote in addition to any other vote he may have.

19. A poll demanded on the election of a chairman, or on a question of adjournment, shall be taken immediately. A poll demanded on any other question shall be taken at such time and in such manner as the chairman of the meeting directs, not being more than [thirty] days after the poll is demanded, and any business other than that upon which a poll has been demanded may proceed pending the taking of the poll. The result of the poll shall be deemed to be the resolution of the meeting at which the poll was demanded.

20. Subject to the provisions of the Act, a resolution in writing signed by all the members entitled to receive notice of and to attend and vote at General Meetings (or being organisations by their duly authorised representatives) shall be as valid and effective as if it had been passed at a General Meeting of the Company duly convened and held. Any such resolution in writing may consist of two or more documents in like form each signed by one or more members.

21. No notice need be given of a poll not taken immediately if the time and the place at which it is to be taken are announced at the meeting at which it is demanded. In other cases at least seven clear days' notice shall be given specifying the time and place at which the poll is to be taken.

Votes of members

22. Subject to Article 18, every member shall have one vote.

23. No member shall be entitled to vote at any General Meeting unless all moneys presently payable by him to the Company have been paid.

24. No objection shall be raised to the qualification of any voter except at the meeting or adjourned meeting at which the vote objected to is tendered, and every vote not disallowed at the meeting shall be valid. Any objection made in due time shall be referred to the chairman whose decision shall be final and conclusive.

25. A vote given or poll demanded by the duly authorised representative of a member organisation shall be valid notwithstanding the previous determination of the authority of the person voting or demanding a poll unless notice of the determination was received by the Company at the Office before the commencement of the meeting or adjourned meeting at which the vote is given or the poll demanded (in the case of a poll taken otherwise than on the same day as the meeting or adjourned meeting) the time appointed for taking the poll.

26. (a) Any member of the Company entitled to attend and vote at a General Meeting shall be entitled to appoint another person (whether a member or not) as his proxy to attend and vote instead of him and any proxy so appointed shall have the same right as the member to speak at the Meeting.

(b) On a poll votes may be given either personally or by proxy.

27. The instrument appointing a proxy shall be in writing under the hand of the appointor or of his attorney duly authorised in writing, or, if the appointor is a corporation, either under seal or under the hand of an officer or attorney duly authorised. A proxy need not be a member of the Company.

28. The instrument appointing a proxy and the power of attorney or other authority, if any, under which it is signed or a notarially certified copy of that power or authority shall be deposited at the Office of the Company or at such other place within the United Kingdom as is specified for that purpose in the notice convening the meeting, not less than forty-eight hours before the time for holding the meeting or adjourned meeting at which the person named in the instrument proposes to vote, or, in the case of a poll, not less than twenty-four hours before the time appointed for the taking of the poll, and in default the instrument of proxy shall not be treated as valid.

29. An instrument appointing a proxy shall be in the following form or a form as near thereto as circumstances admit:

[Limited].

I/We   of   in the County of   being a member/members of the above named Company, hereby appoint   of   or failing him   of   as my/our proxy to vote for me/us on my/our behalf at the (Annual or Extraordinary, as the case may be) General Meeting of the Company to be held on the   day of   19 , and at any adjournment thereof.

Signed this   day of   19 .'

30. Where it is desired to afford members an opportunity of voting for or against a resolution the instrument appointing a proxy shall be in the following form or a form as near thereto as circumstances admit:

[Limited].

I/We   of   in the County of   being a member/members of the above named Company, hereby appoint   of   or failing him   of   as my/our proxy to vote for me/us on my/our behalf at the (Annual or Extraordinary, as the case may be) General Meeting of the Company to be held on the   day of   19   , and at any adjournment thereof.

Signed this   day of   19 .'

This form is to be used *<u>in favour of</u> the resolution.
                              against

Unless otherwise instructed, the proxy will vote as he thinks fit.

*Strike out whichever is not desired

31. The instrument appointing a proxy shall be deemed to confer authority to demand or join in demanding a poll.

32. A vote given in accordance with the terms of an instrument of proxy shall be valid notwithstanding the previous death or insanity of the principal or revocation of the proxy or of the authority under which the proxy was executed, provided that no intimation in writing of such death, insanity or revocation as aforesaid shall have been received by the Company at the Office before the commencement of the meeting or adjourned meeting at which the proxy is used.

Organisations acting by representatives at meetings

33. Any organisation which is a member of the Company may by resolution of its committee or other governing body authorise such person as it thinks fit to act as its representative at any meeting of the Company, and the person so authorised shall be entitled to exercise the same powers on behalf of the organisation which he represents as that organisation could exercise if it were an individual member of the Company.

Management committee

34. The maximum number of the members of the Committee shall be determined by the Company in General Meeting, but unless and until so fixed there shall be no maximum number. The minimum number of the members of the Committee shall be [three].

35. The first members of the Committee shall be those persons named in the statement delivered pursuant to section 10(2) of the Act, who shall be deemed to have been appointed under these Articles. Future members of the Committee shall be appointed as provided subsequently in these Articles.

36. The members of the Committee shall be paid all reasonable out-of-pocket, hotel and other expenses properly incurred by them in attending and returning from meetings of the Committee or General Meetings of the Company or in connection with the business of the Company.

Borrowing powers

37. The Committee may exercise all the powers of the Company to borrow money, and subject always to sections 38 and 39 of the Charities Act 1993 to mortgage or charge its undertaking and property, or any part thereof, and to issue debentures, debenture stock and other securities, whether outright or as security for any debt, liability or obligation of the Company or of any charitable body where such action will directly further the objects of the Company.

Powers and duties of the committee

38. (a) The business of the Company shall be managed by the Committee who may pay all expenses incurred in the formation of the Company, and may exercise all such powers of the Company as are not, by the Act or by these Articles required to be exercised by the Company in General Meeting. Any such requirement may be imposed either by the Act or by these Articles or by regulations made by the Company in General Meeting; but no such regulation shall invalidate any prior act of the Committee which would have been valid if that regulation had not been made.

(b) In the exercise of the aforesaid powers and in the management of the business of a Company, the members of the Committee shall always be mindful that they are charity trustees within the definition of section 97 of the Charities Act 1993 as the persons having the general control and management of the administration of a charity.

39. All cheques and other negotiable instruments, and all receipts for moneys paid to the Company, shall be signed, drawn, accepted, endorsed or otherwise executed, as the case may be, in such manner as the Committee shall from time to time determine provided that all cheques shall be signed by two members of the Committee or one member of the Committee and one authorised signatory.

40. The Committee shall cause minutes to be made:
  (a) of all appointments of officers made by the Committee;
  (b) of the names of the members of the Committee present at each Committee meeting; and
  (c) of all resolutions and proceedings at all meetings of the Company, and of the Committee and of sub-committees.

Disqualification and removal of committee members

41. The office of member of the Committee shall be vacated if the member of the Committee:
  (a) ceases to be a member of the Committee by virtue of any provision in the Act or is disqualified from acting as a member of the Committee by virtue of section 72 of the Charities Act 1993 (or any statutory re-enactment or modification of that provision); or
  (b) becomes incapable by reason of mental disorder, illness or injury of managing and administering his property and affairs; or

(c) resigns his office by written notice to the Company; or
(d) is absent without the permission of the Committee members from all their meetings held within a period of [six] months and the Committee members resolve that his office be vacated; or
(e) is directly or indirectly interested in any contract with the Company and fails to declare the nature of his interest in the manner required by section 317 of the Act.
42. A Committee member shall not vote in respect of any contract in which he is interested or any matter arising thereout, and if he does so vote his vote shall not be counted.

Election of committee members
43. At the first and every subsequent Annual General Meeting of the Company all the members of the Committee shall retire from office.
44. A retiring member of the Committee shall be eligible for re-election [PROVIDED that no member of the Committee shall be eligible for re-election on more than [five] consecutive occasions].
45. The Company at the meeting at which a member of the Committee retires in manner aforesaid may fill the vacated office by electing a person thereto, and in default the retiring member of the Committee shall, if offering himself for re-election, be deemed to have been re-elected, unless at such meeting it is expressly resolved not to fill such vacated office or unless a resolution for the re-election of such member of the Committee shall have been put to the meeting and lost.
46. No person other than a member of the Committee retiring at the meeting shall unless recommended by the Committee be eligible for election to the Committee at any General Meeting unless, not less than [three] nor more than [twenty-one] days before the date set for the meeting, there shall have been left at the Office notice in writing signed by a member qualified to attend and vote at the meeting for which such notice is given, of his intention to propose such person for election, and also notice in writing signed by that person of his willingness to be elected. The notice shall give the particulars of that person which would, if he were so appointed, be required to be included in the register of members of the Committee.
47. Subject to Article 34 the Company may from time to time by ordinary resolution increase or reduce the number of members of the Committee.
48. The Committee shall have the power at any time to appoint any person to be a member of the Committee, either to fill a casual vacancy or as an addition to the existing members but so that the total number of members of the Committee shall not at any time exceed any maximum number fixed in accordance with these Articles. Any member of the Committee so appointed shall hold office only until the next following Annual General Meeting, and shall then be eligible for re-election.
49. The Company may by ordinary resolution, of which special notice has been given in accordance with section 303 of the Act, remove any member of

the Committee before the expiration of his period of office notwithstanding anything in these Articles or in any agreement between the Company and such member. The Company may by ordinary resolution appoint another person in place of a member of the Committee removed under this Article.
50. No person may be appointed as a member of the Committee:
(a) unless he has attained the age of eighteen years;
(b) in circumstances such that, had he already been a member of the Committee, he would have been disqualified from acting under the provisions of Article 41.

Proceedings of the committee

51. The Committee may meet together for the despatch of business, adjourn, and otherwise regulate their meetings, as they think fit. Questions arising at any meeting shall be decided by a majority of votes. In the case of an equality of votes the chair shall have a second or casting vote. A member of the Committee may, and the secretary on the request of a member of the Committee shall, at any time summon a Committee meeting. It shall not be necessary to give notice of a Committee meeting to any member for the time being absent from the United Kingdom.
52. The quorum necessary for the transaction of the business of the Committee may be fixed by the Committee and unless so fixed shall be [one-third] of the membership of the Committee, subject to a minimum of [three].
53. The Committee may act notwithstanding any vacancy in their body, but, if and so long as their number is reduced below the number fixed by or pursuant to these Articles as the necessary quorum of members, the Committee may act for the purpose of increasing the number of members to that number, or of summoning a General Meeting of the Company, but for no other purpose.
54. The Committee may elect a chairman of their meetings and determine the period for which he is to hold office; but, if no such chairman is elected, or if at any meeting the chairman is not present within five minutes after the time appointed for holding the same, the members of the Committee present may choose one of their number to chair the meeting.
55. The Committee may delegate any of their powers to sub-committees consisting of such persons as they think fit; any sub-committee so formed shall conform to any regulations that may be imposed on it by the Committee and shall report all acts and proceedings to the Committee fully and promptly.
56. A sub-committee may elect a chairman of its meetings; if no such chairman is elected, or if at any meeting the chairman is not present within five minutes after the time appointed for holding the same, the members present may choose one of their number to chair the meeting.
57. A sub-committee may meet and adjourn as it thinks proper. Questions arising at any meeting shall be determined by a majority of votes of the members present, and in the case of an equality of votes the chairman shall have a second or casting vote.

58. All acts done by any meeting of the Committee or of a sub-committee, or by any person acting as a member of the Committee shall, notwithstanding that it be afterwards discovered that there was some defect in the appointment of any such member or person acting as aforesaid, or that they or any of them were disqualified, be as valid as if every person had been duly appointed and was qualified to be a member of the Committee.

59. A resolution in writing, signed by all the members of the Committee entitled to receive notice of a Committee meeting, shall be as valid and effectual as if it had been passed at a Committee meeting duly convened and held, and may consist of several documents in like form each signed by one member of the Committee or more.

Secretary

60. Subject to section 283 of the Act, the secretary shall be appointed by the Committee for such term at such remuneration and upon such conditions as the Committee may think fit; and any secretary so appointed may be removed by it: PROVIDED always that no member of the Committee may occupy the salaried position of secretary.

61. A provision of the Act or these Articles requiring or authorising a thing to be done by or to a member of the Committee and the secretary shall not be satisfied by its being done by or to the same person acting both as a member of the Committee and as, or in place of, the secretary.

The seal

62. The Committee shall provide for the safe custody of the seal, if any, which shall only be used by the authority of the Committee or of a sub-committee authorised by the Committee in that behalf and every instrument to which the seal shall be affixed shall be signed by a member of the Committee and shall be countersigned by the secretary or by a second member of the Committee or by some other person appointed by the Committee for that purpose.

Accounts

63. The Committee shall ensure that accounting records are kept in accordance with the provisions of the Act and the Charities Act 1993 as the case may be.

64. The accounting records shall be kept at the Office or, subject to the provisions of the Act, at such other place or places as the Committee thinks fit, and shall always be open to the inspection of the officers of the Company.

65. The Committee shall from time to time determine whether and to what extent and at what times and places and under what conditions or regulations the accounts and books of the Company or any of them shall be open to the inspection of members not being members of the Committee and no member (not being a member of the Committee) shall have any right of inspecting any account or book or document of the Company except as

confirmed by statute or authorised by the Committee or by the Company in General Meeting.

66. The Committee shall from time to time in accordance with the provisions of the Act, cause to be prepared and to be laid before the Company in General Meeting such profit and loss accounts, balance sheets, group accounts (if any) and reports as are referred to in those provisions.

67. A copy of every balance sheet (including every document required by law to be annexed thereto) which is to be laid before the Company in General Meeting, together with a copy of the auditor's report (if any), and the Committee's report, shall not less than twenty-one days before the date of the meeting be sent to every member of the Company and every person entitled to receive notice of General Meetings of the Company.

Audit

68. Auditors shall be appointed and their duties regulated in accordance with the provisions of the Act or the Charities Act 1993 as the case may be.

Annual report

69. The Committee members shall comply with their obligations under the Charities Act 1993 (or any statutory re-enactment or modification of that Act) with regard to the preparation of an annual report and its transmission to the Charity Commissioners.

Annual return

70. The members of the Committee shall comply with their obligations under the Charities Act 1993 (or any statutory re-enactment or modification thereof) with regard to the preparation of an annual return and its transmission to the Charity Commissioners.

Notices

71. Any notice to be given to or by any person pursuant to these Articles shall be in writing except that a notice calling a meeting of the Committee need not be in writing.

72. The Company may give any notice to a member either personally or by sending it by post to him or to his registered address or by leaving it at that address. A member whose registered address is not within the United Kingdom and who gives the Company an address within the United Kingdom at which notices may be given to him shall be entitled to have notices given to him at that address, but otherwise no such member shall be entitled to receive any notice from the Company.

73. Notice of every General Meeting shall be given in any manner hereinbefore authorised to:
   (a) every member except those members who (having no registered address within the United Kingdom) have not supplied to the Company an address within the United Kingdom for giving of notices to them;

(b) every person being a legal personal representative or a trustee in bankruptcy of a member where the member but for his death or bankruptcy would be entitled to receive notice of the meeting;
(c) the auditor for the time being of the Company; and
(d) each member of the Committee.

No other person shall be entitled to receive notices of General Meetings.

74. A member present in person at any General Meeting of the Company shall be deemed to have received notice of the meeting and, where necessary, of the purposes for which it was called.

75. Proof that an envelope containing a notice was properly addressed, prepaid and posted shall be conclusive evidence that the notice was given. A notice shall be deemed to be given at the expiration of forty-eight hours after the envelope containing it was posted.

Indemnity

76. Subject to the provisions of the Act every member of the Committee or other officer or auditor of the Company shall be indemnified out of the assets of the Company against any liability incurred by him in that capacity in defending any proceedings, whether civil or criminal, in which judgment is given in his favour or in which he is acquitted or in connection with any application under section 727 of the Act in which relief is granted to him by the court from liability from negligence, default, breach of duty or breach of trust in relation to the affairs of the Company.

Investments

77. The Committee shall have power from time to time to appoint on such terms (including provision for reasonable remuneration) as the Committee shall at their discretion think fit any person or persons who the Committee reasonably believe to be qualified by his ability in the practical experience of financial matters to be the Company's investment adviser for the purpose of advising the Committee in relation to the investments of the Company and managing such investments. The Committee may make such arrangement as they think fit for any investments of the Company or income from those investments to be held by a corporate body as the Company's nominee and pay reasonable and proper remuneration to any corporate body acting as such nominee.

In making such arrangements as described above the Committee shall ensure that:
(a) the terms of any delegation of power are clearly stated in writing and contain adequate control mechanisms and
(b) such delegation extends only to such things as the Committee have power to do and
(c) the terms of any such delegation are strictly enforced by the Committee.

Dissolution

78. Clause 7 of the Memorandum of Association relating to the winding up and dissolution of the Company shall have effect as if the provisions thereof were repeated in these Articles.

Rules or bye laws

79. The Committee may from time to time make such Rules or Bye Laws as they may deem necessary or convenient for the proper conduct and management of the Company and for the purpose of prescribing classes of and conditions of membership, and in particular but without prejudice to the generality of the foregoing, they may by such Rules or Bye Laws regulate:

(a) the admission and classification of members of the Company, and the rights and privileges of such members, and the conditions of membership and the terms on which members may resign or have their membership terminated and the entrance fees, subscriptions and other fees or payments to be made by members.

(b) the conduct of members of the Company in relation to one another, and to the Company's employees.

(c) the setting aside of the whole or any part or parts of the Company's premises at any particular time or times or for any particular purpose or purposes.

(d) the procedure at General Meetings and meetings of the Committee and sub-committees in so far as such procedure is not regulated by these Articles.

(e) and, generally, all such matters as are commonly the subject matter of Company rules.

80. The Company in General Meeting shall have power to alter or repeal the Rules or Bye Laws and to make additions to them and the Committee shall adopt such means as they deem sufficient to bring to the notice of members of the Company all such Rules or Bye Laws, which, so long as they shall be in force, shall be binding on all members of the Company. PROVIDED, nevertheless, that no Rule or Bye Law shall be inconsistent with, or shall affect or repeal anything contained in, the Memorandum or Articles of Association of the Company.

APPENDIX 3

WHERE TO FIND FURTHER INFORMATION

Association of Charity Officers
Beechwood House, Wylotts Manor,
Potters Bar, Hertfordshire
Tel: 01707 651777 Fax: 01707 660477

Association of Charitable Foundations:
4 Bloomsbury Square, London WC2A 2RL
Tel: 0171–404 1338 Fax: 0171–831 3881

Charities Advisory Trust:
Radius Works, Back Lane, London NW3 1HL
Tel: 0171–435 6523 Fax: 0171–431 3739

Charities Aid Foundation:
Kings Hill Avenue, West Malling, Kent ME19 4TA
Tel: 01732 520000 Fax: 01732 520001

Charity Finance Directors Group:
Link Building, Tanners Lane, Ilford, Essex IG6 1QG
Tel: 0181–503 9217 Fax: 0181-503 9291

Charities Official Investment Fund:
St Alphage House, 2 Fore Street, London EC2Y 5AQ
Tel: 0171–588 1815 Fax: 0171–588 6291

Charity Commission:
St Alban's House, 57/60 Haymarket, London SW1Y 4QX
Tel: 0171–210 4556
2nd Floor, 20 Kings Parade, Queen's Dock, Liverpool L3 4DQ
Tel: 0151–703 1500
Woodfield House, Tangier, Taunton, Somerset TA1 4BL
Tel: 01823–345000

Companies House:
Crown Way, Maindy, Cardiff CF4 3UZ
Tel: 01222 388588 Fax: 01222 380900

The Directory of Social Change:
Federation House, Hope Street, Liverpool L1 9BW
Tel: 0151–708 0117 Fax: 0151–708 0139
24 Stephenson Way, London NW1 2DP
Tel: 0171–209 0902 Fax: 0171–209 4130

Home Office Voluntary Services Unit:
50 Queen Anne's Gate, London SW1H 9AT
Tel: 0171-273 2483 Fax: 0171-273 2190

The Institute of Charity Fundraising Managers:
Market Towers, 1 Nine Elms Lane, London SW8 5NQ
Tel: 0171–627 3436 Fax 0171–627 3508

The Institute of Chartered Secretaries and Administrators:
16 Park Crescent, London W1N 4AH
Tel: 0171–580 4741 Fax: 0171–753 0702

National Council for Voluntary Organisations:
Regent's Wharf, 8 All Saints Street, London N1 9RL
Tel: 0171–713 6161 Fax: 0171–713 6000

National Lottery Charities Board:
7th Floor, St Vincent House, 30 Orange Street, London WC2H 7HH
Tel: 0171–747 5299 Fax: 0171 747 5214

Northern Ireland Council for Voluntary Action:
127 Ormeau Road, Belfast BT7 1SH
Tel: 01232–321 224 Fax: 01232–438 350

Scottish Council for Voluntary Organizations:
18–19 Claremont Crescent, Edinburgh EH7 4QD
Tel: 0131–556 3882 Fax: 0131–556 0279

Trustee Register:
Bedford House, Madeira Walk, Windsor, Berkshire SL4 1EU
Tel: 01753 868277 Fax: 01753 841688

Volunteer Centre UK:
Carriage Row, 183 Eversholt Street, London NW1 1BU
Tel: 0171–388 9888 Fax: 0171–383 0448

Wales Council for Voluntary Action:
Lys Ifor, Crescent Road, Caerphilly, Mid Glamorgan CR8 1XL
Tel: 01222 869224 Fax 01222 860-627

INDEX

Accounts
    accounting records   13, 18
    annual statutory   19, 142
    audit of   14, 44, 145
    charitable companies   18, 145
    charities with annual income of less than £100,000   142
    charities with annual income in excess of £100,000   143
    circulation of statutory accounts and reports   19
    copies to be made available on request   14
    filing requirements   14, 43, 144
    financial thresholds   142
    management accounting   139–142
    records   13, 18, 41
    regulations   14, 36, 142
    SOFA   139, 143
    SORP   13, 137, 141–143
    trustees' annual report   143, 144
Administration
    best practice   3
    'boardroom' practice, a code   73
    committee meetings   69
    competent, need for   3
Advisers
    categories of   61
    honorary   55
    investment   155, 172
    retention of   61
    selection of   61
    specialist   60
    status of   98

Agenda
    agenda papers   88, 89
    items of business   87, 88
Alterations to constitution
    review of, by secretary   8
    charitable company, of   81
    unincorporated charity, of   78
Annual reports
    annual general meetings, consideration at   91
    filing with Commission   14, 143
    preparation and contents of   14, 143, 144
Annual return
    charitable company   19
    registered charity   23
Audit
    management   138
    statutory   14, 44, 145
Auditing requirements
    auditor, qualification of   145
    independent examination   14, 145
    internal controls   138
    specific funds   143
    statutory regulations   142

Bequests   104, 141
Budgetary control   137, 138
Business plan   108, 137

Capital fund-raising   108
Cash control   138, 139
Central register of charities
    computerisation of register   24
    registration with Commission   41

Chairman
  committee 68
  governance and 76
  honorary officer 45
Charitable companies
  accounting records 18
  advantages of incorporation 77
  alteration of objects 82
  annual return 19
  articles of association 80, 161–173
  audit requirements 145
  consent of Commission to
      amendments to 82
  disadvantages of incorporation 78
  ensuring compliance with governing
      document 81
  insolvent, trading while 43
  letterhead 20, 21
  meetings of members 91, 92
  memorandum 80, 57–160
  name, direction for change of 12
  stationery 20, 21
Charitable Institutions (Fund-Raising)
    Regulations 1994 103
Charities (Accounts and Reports)
    Regulations 1995 14, 136, 142
Charities legislation
  accountability of trustees 11
  accounting records 13, 18
  annual accounts, filing of 14
  annual accounting statements 13
  annual reports 14, 24
  annual returns 23, 24
  commercial participator 110
  land transactions 13, 94, 96–99
  professional fund-raisers 108, 109
  power of Commission to institute
      inquiries 13
  requirement to change name of
      charity 12
  small charities 39
  supervisory role of Commission 12
  trustees, disqualification of 37, 52
Charity administration
  committees 68
  investment 39, 155, 172
  legislation 22
Charity Commission
  assistance and supervision by 12
  filing accounts with 14, 143, 144
  information, power to request 13
  inquiries by 13
  registration with 41
  remuneration, power to authorise
      payment 47
  supervisory role of 12
Charity shops, rating of 98
Charity trading companies 106–8
Committees
  chairman, appointment of 68
  composition 68
  constitution of 66
  efficient conduct of business 69
  forming 65
  functional 66
  governing body, role of 66
  legal aspects 68
  quorum 69
  rationale 65
  reasons for establishing 65
  selection 68
  size 67
  terms of reference 67
Companies, charity trading 106–108
Company Directors Disqualification Act
    (1986) 52, 54
Compliance
  Charity Commission, supervisory role
      of 12
  charitable company, additional
      requirements 16
  maintenance of accounting
      records 13, 18
  routine obligations under companies
      legislation 15
Constitution
  charitable company of 80–82
  compliance with 78, 81
  consent of Charity Commission to
      amendments 79
  points to check in review 79, 81
  unincorporated association of 78
Consultant
  agreement with fund-raising 108,
      109
  choice of 61
Contents Insurance 100
Contract of employment 115–118

Contracts, terms and conditions 23
Covenant, deed of
   dates in 114
   definition 105
   higher-rate tax payers 104
   specimen 114
   tax efficiency 104

Director/trustees
   appointment 50
   compensation for loss of office 54
   criminal law 54
   definition 49
   general duty of care 50
   letter on appointment 63
   liability of 52
   persons disqualified 52
   register of and inspection 17
   removal of 54
   retirement of 53
   shadow 49, 51
   qualification of 50
Documents
   company name, appearance on 21
   power of Commission to order production of 13

Elective regime 15, 92
Employees
   health and safety, duties of 133
   responsibility of 55
   senior 35
   trustees and 57
   volunteers and 59
Employment
   constructive dismissal 125
   contract of 115–118
   deductions from wages 118
   disciplinary procedures 118–120
   dismissal,
      fact of 125
      giving reasons for 121
   fair reason for dismissal 126–129
   gross misconduct 121
   itemised pay statements 118
   obligations of employers 116, 130–133
   pregnancy 128
   references and testimonials 122
   sick pay 119
   written statement of main terms 117, 118
Employment legislation
   health and safety 130–134
   illegal immigrants 123
   redundancy 122
   volunteers 134, 135
   written statement of terms 117, 118
Employment Rights Act 1996 117, 118, 120

Fair dismissal 126–129
Financial and management accounting
   basic principles 139
   capital funding 141, 142
   cash control 139, 140
   expenditure on primary charitable objectives 141
   sources of income 140, 141
Financial management and control
   annual statutory accounts 142
   auditing requirements 145
   management control procedures 14, 137
   statutory audit/independent examination 145
Fire insurance 99
Forming a charity
   incorporation, advantages and disadvantages 77, 78
   registration 41
Freehold property
   acquisition of 94, 96
   funding purchase of 97
Fund-raising
   appeal plan 108
   capital 108
   charity trading companies 106–8
   commercial participator 110
   consultants 109
   covenant 104
   fund-raising agreements, provisions to be included 111, 112
   legacies 103, 104
   lotteries 106
   professional fund-raiser 109

questions to ask consultant or fund-raiser   109

Governance
  'boardroom' practice, a code   73
  Cadbury recommendations   74
  governing document, review of   72
  minutes, preparation of   6, 7, 74, 89, 90
  ostensible authority of secretary   71
  principles of good   75
  secretary, and   2, 8, 75
Health and Safety Executive   133
Health and Safety
  common law duties   130
  employee's duties   133
  employers' duty to employees   130–133
  employers' duty to others   133
  enforcement   133
  legislation   131
  recording of accidents   134
  secretary and   22
  sources of law   130
Honorary advisers   55
Honorary officers
  chairman   45
  definition   44
  president   44
  secretary   45
  treasurer   45
  vice-chairman   45
  vice-president   44

Income
  restricted   143
  sources   140
Incorporation, advantages and disadvantages   77, 78
Indemnity   42, 156, 172
Independent examination   145
Information, powers of Commission to request   13
Insolvency Act 1986   43, 49, 52, 54
Insurance
  advisers   101
  buildings   100
  checklist   101
  contents   100
  duty of trustees   99
  employers' liability   100
  property   99
  public liability   101
  secretary and   9
  trustee liability   43
Investment
  income from   141
  powers of, by trustees   39

Job security
  notice by employer   120
  payment in lieu of notice   120

Land
  acquisition of   94, 97, 98
  dealing with   13
  disposal of   99
  freehold   22, 96
  holding trustees   35
  leasehold   22, 42, 96
  licence   94, 97
  mortgage of   97
  transfer of title   43
Landlord and Tenant Act 1954   97, 99
Leases   22, 42, 96, 97
Legacies
  accounting for   141
  forms of bequest   104
  potential   103
  will, form of   104
Legal 'healthcheck'
  employment   22
  governing document   22
  health and safety   22
  legacies   23
  property   22
  terms and conditions of contract   23
Legislation
  discrimination   125
  employment   117, 118
  fund-raising   103
  health and safety   131
  lotteries   105
Liability insurance
  employers'   100
  trustees'   43

Lotteries
  legislation 105
  private 106
  small 106
  society 106

Management
  accounts 137
  audit 138, 139
  committee, by 65, 66
  employees and 55, 56
  financial control procedures 137, 138
  specialist advisers and consultants 60–62
Meetings
  annual general meetings 91
  agenda 87
  agenda papers 89
  availability of members 84
  'boardroom' practice, a code 73
  briefing notes 88
  charitable company, additional requirements 90
  decisions, implementing 6
  director/trustees, of 90
  extraordinary general meetings 92
  frequency and timing 84, 85, 91
  governing document 85
  law of 85, 86, 87
  members of a charitable company, of 91
  minute books 18
  minutes 18, 74, 89, 90
  nature and volume of work between 84
  notice of 86
  secretarial support at 87
  secretary's role at 89
  secretary's role before 87
  staff availability 85
  terms of reference for 67
Members
  annual accounts, right to receive 19
  cessation of membership 149, 150, 161, 162
  general meetings, notice of 86
  register of members 16
  requisition of EGM 92
  statutory books and records, inspection of 16, 17, 18
Memorandum of charitable company 80, 157–160
Minutes
  books of 18
  committee meetings 67
  contents of 90
  location of 18
  preparation of 6, 7, 74, 89, 90
  requirement to keep 18
Mortgages
  register of charges and mortgages 18
  inspection 19

Names
  correspondence of charitable companies 20
  power of Commission to require change 12
  registered charities, of 20
Notices
  committee meetings, of 69
  meetings of director/trustees 90
  meetings of members, of 86

Objects
  charitable company, of 157
  unincorporated association, of 147
Offences
  Charities Act 1993 24
  companies legislation 25, 92

Panorama case 71
Permanent endowment 2, 143
Personnel administration
  discrimination 124, 128
  division of responsibility 58
  employee responsibility 55
  health and safety 22, 130–134
  redundancy 122
  references 122
  senior employees 55
  termination on notice 120
  written statement of main terms 117, 118
Powers
  charitable companies 157–159

trustees   38, 39
unincorporated associations   147–149
Property
  acquisition of   94, 96
  assignment of lease   96
  disposal of   99
  funding acquisition of   97
  insurance   99
  leases   96, 97
  licences   97
  mortgaging   97
  permitted use   94
  planning permission   95
  rating   98
  survey   95
  transfer on retirement of trustee   43
Public liability insurance   101

Quorum
  charitable company   90, 163, 166
  size of committee and   69
  unincorporated association   86, 150, 153

Rates   98
Rehabilitation of Offenders Act 1974   37
Register of members
  maintenance of   16
  inspection of   16
Remuneration of trustees
  basic principles   46
  Commission's power to authorise payment   47
  directors of an associated trading company   49
  expenses   49
  factors to be taken into account   47, 48
  honorarium   48
  principles   46
  professionally qualified trustees, payments to   48
Restricted funds   143
Retirement of trustees   43, 53
Returns
  annual to Charity Commission   23
  annual to Registrar of Companies   19, 20

Secretary
  accounting and taxation   9
  administrative support for trustees   5
  authority of   71
  communication by, internal and external   6
  compliance, and   8
  co-ordination by   8
  core duties and responsibilities of   5
  custodian of governing document,   8
  governance and   8, 75
  honorary officer, as   45
  increasing importance of   71
  legal guidance and advice from   7
  liability of   72
  members and supporters, communication with   6
  minutes, preparation of   6, 7, 74, 89, 90
  meetings, administration of   64
  officer of charitable company, as   72
  ostensible authority of   71
  requirements of company law   4
  role of   2, 4
  status of   70
  statutory registers, maintenance of   15, 72
Selection
  advisers, of   61
  committee members, of   68
Small charities   39
Specialist advisers and consultants
  categories of   61
  requirement for   60
  purpose of   60
  selection of   61
Statement of Recommended Practice SORP   13, 131, 141–143
Stationery
  charitable company, of   20
  letterhead   20
  name of charity on   21
  names of director/trustees   21
  registered charity, of   20

Trustee Investments Act 1961   39
Trustees
  accountability of   11

Trustees (*continued*)
  accounting records, maintenance
    of   18, 41
  annual report   14, 143, 144
  appointment of   36
  approach to role   38
  breach of trust   41
  Commission's power to advise   42
  compliance with aims and objectives,
    by   41
  conflict of interest, no   40
  custodian   35
  delegation by   38
  director/trustees   49, 50
  disqualification from acting as   37,
    52
  duties of   39–41, 50
  employees and   57
  financial and administrative
    control   40
  holding   35
  honorarium   48
  indemnity   42
  insolvent trading   43, 52
  insurance   43
  investment powers of   39
  letter on appointment   62–64
  land, dealing with by   13, 96, 97
  leases by   42, 96
  liability of   41–43, 96
  personal qualities of   36
  powers of   38, 39
  property sales by   96, 97
  protection of assets by   39
  qualification of   36
  re-appointment of   37
  registration by   41
  removal of   37, 54
  remuneration of   46, 47
  responsibility of   55
  retirement of   37, 43, 53
  status of   35
  transfer of title by   43
  wrongful trading by   43, 52

Unfair dismissal   123–129

Volunteers
  employees and   59
  expenses   134
  insurance and   135
  status of   134

Wills   104
Winding up   77, 80
Wrongful trading   43, 52